SEARCHING FOR SERAFIM

SEARCHING *for* SERAFIM

THE LIFE AND LEGACY OF SERAFIM "JOE" FORTES

RUBY SMITH DÍAZ

ARSENAL PULP PRESS
VANCOUVER

SEARCHING FOR SERAFIM

ARSENAL PULP PRESS
Suite 202 – 211 East Georgia St.
Vancouver, BC V6A 1Z6
Canada
arsenalpulp.com

The publisher gratefully acknowledges the support of the Canada Council for the Arts and the British Columbia Arts Council for its publishing program and the Government of Canada and the Government of British Columbia (through the Book Publishing Tax Credit Program) for its publishing activities.

British Columbia | British Columbia Arts Council An agency of the Province of British Columbia | Canada Council for the Arts Conseil des arts du Canada | Canada

Arsenal Pulp Press acknowledges the xʷməθkʷəy̓əm (Musqueam), Sḵwx̱wú7mesh (Squamish), and səlilwətaɬ (Tsleil-Waututh) Nations, custodians of the traditional, ancestral, and unceded territories where our office is located. We pay respect to their histories, traditions, and continuous living cultures and commit to accountability, respectful relations, and friendship.

Cover design by Rebecca Poulin in collaboration with Jazmin Welch
Cover photo by W. Chapman, City of Vancouver Archives AM336-S3-2-: CVA 677-441; colourized by Rebecca Poulin
Back cover photo by W.T. Dalton, City of Vancouver Archives AM54-S4-1-L-12-: L-12-37
Text design by Jazmin Welch
Edited by Catharine Chen
Proofread by Alison Strobel
Indexed by Catharine Chen

Printed and bound in Canada

Library and Archives Canada Cataloguing in Publication:
Title: Searching for Serafim : the life and legacy of Serafim "Joe" Fortes / Ruby Smith Díaz.
Names: Smith Díaz, Ruby, author.
Description: Includes bibliographical references and index.
Identifiers: Canadiana (print) 20240445953 | Canadiana (ebook) 20240447417 | ISBN 9781551529752 (softcover) | ISBN 9781551529769 (EPUB)
Subjects: LCSH: Fortes, Joe, 1863–1922. | LCSH: Lifeguards—British Columbia—Vancouver—Biography. | LCSH: Racism against Black people—British Columbia—Vancouver—History. | LCSH: Vancouver (B.C.)—Biography. | CSH: Trinidadian Canadians—British Columbia—Vancouver—Biography. | LCGFT: Biographies.
Classification: LCC GV838.F67 S65 2025 | DDC 797.20092—dc23

Para mi mamá y al cofrecito de trigo que nunca nos abandonó

En vano se echa la red ante los ojos de los que tienen alas.

—GABRIELA MISTRAL

To be a Negro in this country and to be relatively conscious is to be in a rage almost all the time.

—JAMES BALDWIN

CONTENTS

11 INTRODUCTION

17 CHAPTER 1 Querencia

23 CHAPTER 2 He Always Followed the Sea

35 CHAPTER 3 All Crab Find Dey Hole

51 CHAPTER 4 Reading Between the Lines of White Supremacy

61 CHAPTER 5 Quantifying Melanin

71 CHAPTER 6 Joe Fortes, Model Negro Citizen

83 CHAPTER 7 On Love and Being Loved

103 CHAPTER 8 Legacy

115 CHAPTER 9 Soliloquy for Serafim

125 ACKNOWLEDGMENTS

127 NOTES

134 BIBLIOGRAPHY

135 INDEX

INTRODUCTION

Cattle horn never too heavy for him to carry.

—TRINIDADIAN PROVERB

I first came across Serafim Joseph Fortes's story during a Black History Month art challenge by Robert Liu-Trujillo on February 6, 2022. The challenge was to depict a Black or African American person, group, or place of significance using any art medium desired.

Searching for inspiration, I dove into the City of Vancouver Archives' online portal, eager to see what I would find under the search term "Black Canadians." Disappointingly, only a handful of images popped up on my screen. I stalled for a moment, playing the dangerous game of remembering other terms that have historically been used for Black Canadians. Finally deciding on "Negro," I hit Backspace and typed it in. The search term only returned a couple more images. How could this be? Out of the thousands of images in the archive—of roads, old houses, posters for events of yesteryear, and Expo 86 memories—only a handful of Black individuals were deemed worthy of photographing and archiving at the turn of the century?

Frustrated, I typed in my original search term again and, this time, focused on viewing the sparse images as most precious items allowing me a window into the past. I scrolled through photographs from the turn of the century, glimpsing "unidentified" Black Canadians in all kinds of landscapes and demeanours, wondering what their lives were like and what circumstances had unfolded for them to be part of the select few able to access a photographer and, furthermore, to wind up in the archives. An image flickered across my screen of a stout, broad-chested, dark-skinned man in shorts and a tank top named Joe Fortes, smiling on the shore of a beach. A couple more clicks revealed the gentle and familiar smile of Barbara Howard, international track star and the first Black teacher to be hired by the Vancouver School Board—I taught Vancouver youth about her during Hogan's Alley history tours. Then another image of Joe Fortes, body outstretched, sporting a striped bathing outfit with shorts and diving headfirst into the water. Another click: Fielding Spotts, one of the first Black people in Vancouver, a peaceful yet focused gaze beneath a wide-brimmed straw hat and broad shoulders in a weathered and stained pinstriped suit. Then another of Joe Fortes, this time wearing a top hat and a full suit, standing in front of a giant boulder. I pressed on, struck by how many images there were of this man, Joe Fortes. Who was he? And why was he documented so much more than others in the Black community? The next photograph of him transported me into another world: dressed to the nines, standing with hands on hips in front of a white canvas tent surrounded by tall trees and lush salal bushes. Carefully assembled planks of wood form a deck in front of his tent, and on top of the planks is a large round table graced with a white linen cloth and set with a silver teapot, awaiting visitors. His air of gravitas—at ease with himself, the land, and the photographer—drew me in. I knew right away that this image would be my muse.

Serafim Fortes, more commonly known as "Joe" Fortes, was Vancouver's first lifeguard. He lived at Íỳel̓shn (English Bay) for most of his life, until his death in 1922. Originally from Trinidad, he was credited with saving the lives of more than one hundred people over the span of his career, and he seemingly gained the esteem of the entire city; there was unprecedented attendance at his funeral, with Vancouverites standing shoulder to shoulder in the streets to bid him farewell.

I began to colourize his photo, my pen strokes highlighting the linens hung to dry on a clothesline next to his canvas tent, then I slowly moved my pen across the tablet screen to reveal the wood grain of the chairs next to the linen-covered table. I took breaks to sip hibiscus tea and read more about his life. Memorial posts about Serafim on social media sparked hundreds of comments—some as recent as a few days back—from Vancouver residents recounting how he had taught their grandparents to swim and how wonderful a man he was. I was struck by his enduring legacy. As I continued colourizing his photograph, I wondered how similar our experiences as Afrocaribeños living in Vancouver are. Did he have trouble finding sorrel out here? Did he know any other Black people in the city? Was he really so loved? How could he have been so loved by so many in a time of active segregation and white supremacist violence? And why did he never go back home to La Trinidad? I gazed at his eyes, looking back at me from the screen, knowing, understanding. It's the last thing I remember from that night.

The next morning, I woke up to sunlight pouring through my basement suite window, shocked to discover my tablet still in my hand, yesterday's T-shirt and jeans uncomfortably twisted on my body. Disoriented, I grabbed my phone to look at the time and flicked away the stack of notifications lighting up my screen. There was still time to make my first meeting. I hurriedly changed out of my wrinkled clothes, put the kettle on, and took my first social media scroll of the day. To my astonishment, Serafim's image filled my phone screen. Exactly one hundred years ago to the day, Serafim Joe Fortes had passed. Goosebumps ran over my entire body. How was it that I had become so entranced with Serafim and his story exactly one hundred years later, seemingly out of nowhere? Was it just a weird coincidence?

Part of me believes that some sort of veil lifted for me to connect with him that night, as a fellow Afro Latine in Vancouver, separated only by time. Even months after the Black History Month art challenge, I couldn't shake the unanswered questions or the eerie feeling that there was something in his story he wanted *me* to tell. Something that hadn't been told before that had been lost to the passage of time. Over the next year, I scoured newspaper and online articles, voraciously reading anything I could get my hands on to help me understand more about who he was.

The more I find out about him, the more I realize that there is a lot about Serafim Fortes we will never know; his motivations, his heartaches, his fears, his sorrows—all are lost to time. There is nobody alive who can tell us about their first-hand experiences with him. Although some direct quotes from him exist in newspaper archives, I have to take them with a grain of salt, knowing that the white supremacist context he was living in meant that only white people were writing about him and that it was never fully safe for him to share all of himself with the outside world. Just like me, Serafim probably often found himself self-monitoring his tone, what he shared about himself, and whom he shared his innermost thoughts with. Perhaps he never shared his full self. And if this is true, then the "Joe" Fortes we know today has largely been created by the white colonial imagination.

As a fellow Afro Latine person, I hope to unravel this mirage of Serafim created by the white imagination and to bring to light aspects of his life that have perhaps not been previously considered. At the same time, I want to draw attention to the many contradictions I perceive about his life and his loyalties. This work is, in itself, reclaiming history.

For the purposes of honouring his legacy, in this book I will be referring to "Joe" Fortes by his first name, Serafim. This name was given to him at birth by his Latina mother. I also choose to write his name in the original Spanish spelling, *Serafim*, rather than the anglicized *Seraphim*, as in the sole surviving document with his signature on it, he signed his name "Serafim."

The only time I use the name "Joe" in my writing is to reflect the white gaze and the white imagination at the time. It is not clear why Serafim became known as simply "Joe." Authors Lisa Anne Smith and Barbara Rogers speculate that his name, meaning the "highest ranking of the Christian angelic hierarchy ... [conjuring] up images of gentle, white-winged angels with glowing halos," perhaps "did not serve [him] well in certain circles."[1] Personally, I believe it was easy for white settlers to use his middle name to latch on to the popular minstrel song of the era "Old Black Joe." Whatever the reason may be, I choose to call him by his own name as a form of resistance. It is an all-too-common experience for migrants to have their names changed without consent by white Canadians out of comfort and laziness. I refuse to continue this practice in my work.

His name was Serafim.

Ruby and Serafim standing side by side at Íy̓el̓shn, one century apart. | Digital collage by Ruby Smith Díaz using image of the author by Keith William Miller, as well as a photo of Serafim Fortes from the City of Vancouver Archives

1 QUERENCIA

Like Serafim Fortes, I am from sugar cane, from cacao, from árboles de café. I am from cilantro and mañanitas on your birthday, and té de menta when your stomach is sick. When I tell his story, I cannot skim over the history that made him who he was and shaped the way he thought. For many who have not had to prove their existence in a white dominant society, these details are often meaningless; they have been left out of articles and books written about Serafim's life. These are not meaningless for me, nor for millions like me. On the contrary, these details are the pillars of his story as a man of mixed ancestry from Trinidad. In telling his story, I reveal a part of my own.

Many a night I have caught my mind wandering through the towering skyscrapers and wet pavement of Vancouver streets, the same streets that Serafim may have wandered over a hundred years ago. Under the glow of the same moon, I lengthen my stride, catching up with the first steps my mother took under moonlight on Turtle Island, free of the toque de queda (curfew) that she left behind in Chile. Just like her, I walk the streets at midnight for no reason other than to feel the light of freedom on my cheek. With my callused fingers, I trace the knotted cedar tree roots exposed through concrete, admiring their refusal to be forgotten. As I honour the cedar roots, I call to mind my father's lineage, who survived their kidnapping from the African continent to Caribbean shores and never forgot their songs or traditions. Somewhere in my body's story lives the

DNA of someone in my family who survived that journey and made it to Jamaica, held hostage in the name of profit. Somewhere on another slave ship, on another shore, the ancestors of Serafim arrived, also held hostage. My mind wanders often, getting entangled in time, imagining what it would be like to wander the streets in shoes like mine, in a different time.

A different time, like in 1498, when a lost Italian navigator by the name of Cristoforo Colombo came across the island of Kairi in the Caribbean Sea, just north of modern-day Venezuela. Lush tropical vegetation and an abundance of wildlife surrounded its three mountain ranges, creating a beautiful homeland for the Taíno and Kalinago peoples. There was melodic uproar in the trees, marking the presence of bountiful avian diversity; ocean waves washed over rock, keeping time with the moon. These bountiful homelands would never be the same after Colombo's accidental arrival.

Enacting the Doctrine of Discovery through the Papal Bull of 1493, Colombo stole the lands of Kairi in the name of the King of Spain and renamed it La Trinidad, effectively dispossessing thousands of inhabitants on the island and enslaving these nations for the profit of European Christian kings. The first enslaved Africans were brought to Kairi's shores in 1606, and Spain continued to amass riches through the theft of natural resources and the forced labour and torture of enslaved African peoples. This violent cycle would continue into the 1800s, even after the Spanish were surrounded by British warships and forced to cede the stolen lands. It did not matter to either power that human beings were trafficked, tortured, and killed. What mattered was who had control of the land and who could amass wealth the quickest.

[Daylight come and me wan go home[2]*]*

Somewhere in this truth lies the tragic irony of being ripped away from your own lush homelands an ocean away, surviving months and months in the belly of a ship—lying in your own feces, mourning your dead while chained to their bodies, wishing for death or for this misery to somehow end—only to arrive in another lush tropical paradise to be sold, enslaved, and have this same cursed story repeat for generation upon generation, for over three hundred years. Somewhere among these truths is the tragic irony of calling the lush tropical paradise that you and your ancestors were enslaved to "home."

[Daylight come and me wan go home]

This story unfolded violently again and again throughout the Caribbean, North America, and South America and facilitated the creation of most modern states, with stolen lands and the enslavement of Indigenous and African peoples as their economic foundation. Only in 2023 was the Doctrine of Discovery rescinded by the Vatican, following another wave of protest by Indigenous communities during the Pope's visit to Canada. Ground-penetrating radar has now confirmed what Indigenous communities in Canada have always known about: the presence of thousands of children's bodies at residential schools run by the Roman Catholic Church. These children were ripped away from their families and brought to residential schools across Canada, starting as early as the 1600s and continuing into the 1990s. At the time of this writing, it is confirmed that at least 4,100 children died as a result of illness, neglect, abuse, or suicide connected to residential schools, but more bodies continue to be uncovered, and many more will never be accounted for due to "lost" documents, poor record keeping, and the withholding of documents by the Roman Catholic Church.[3]

[Daylight come and me wan go home]

Serafim Joseph Fortes was born amid these parallel stories of dispossession and enslavement on the beautiful island of Kairi around 1865.[†] At birth, he was anointed by the rivers and swamps of the island and grew up embraced by the coral reef that crowns its majestic shore. He was born free, a mere thirty years after slavery was abolished across the so-called British Empire.

Just like my father, Serafim's father was descended from enslaved kin. He was likely born on the cusp of abolition in the British colonies around 1834, meaning that the difference of only a few years spared him the fate of becoming the property of a human trafficker for his lifetime. Archival records from Kairi simply cite his occupation as "farmer." Given the continued British colonial rule over the island after 1834, there likely were few to little economic opportunities for Serafim's father besides working on a sugar cane, coffee, or cacao plantation, the primary export industries at the time.

Serafim's mother, just like my mother, was a Latina. There is much speculation as to whether his mother was of Spanish or Portuguese descent. Because Serafim is listed in the Vancouver Census as speaking both Spanish and English, and because his surviving pieces of writing are in a mix of Spanish and English, I feel it is safe to assume that Serafim's mother was not of Portuguese origin. However, just as likely as his mother being of Spanish origin is the strong possibility that she was from Venezuela, given its eleven-kilometre distance from the coast of Trinidad and the history of migration between the two land masses.

As an Afro Latino, Serafim likely grew up hearing Spanish, English, and Patois in his home and community. One of two surviving documents of his writing, on yellowed and tattered paper, filed away at the Vancouver Archives shows his cursive in a mix of both Spanish and English, with

† Serafim's exact birth year is unclear; some sources point to 1865 and others to 1863. This uncertainty opens to the door to what MarieClaire Graham calls "speculative archiving," a speculative methodological approach to restoring silenced Black voices in the official record. (MarieClaire Graham, "Imagining the Archive: Speculation as a Tool of Archival Reconstruction" [MA thesis, City University of New York, 2019], https://academicworks.cuny.edu/gc_etds/3189/.)

neither language written very proficiently. Perhaps Serafim learned to write cursive as a child, practising from the Silabario grammar book just like I did, occasionally interjecting diptóngos in English and Patois.

In one of my imaginings, the edges of his schoolbooks catch dominoes slamming on kitchen tables and interrupting painstakingly shaped cursive, while the ruled lines are infused with roti, cilantro, and discipline. In another imagining, Serafim's father, exhausted after a back-breaking day on the sugar cane plantation, sings a kaiso tune to his son as he sits on the porch underneath a kapok tree, cussing out a master who forced his people to labour to death, belting out the spirit of rebellion in a premonition of the Canboulay riots.

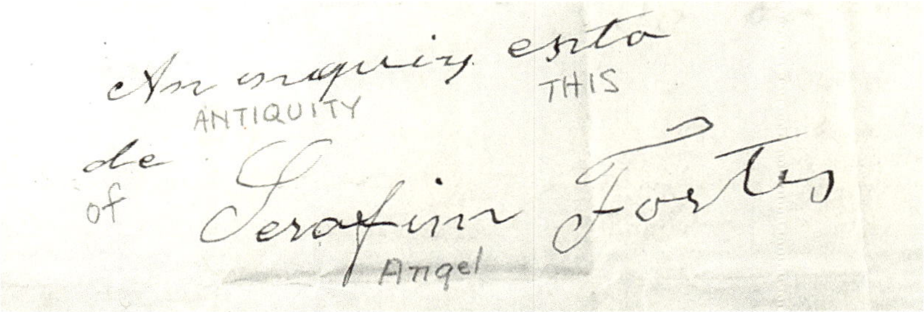

One of only two surviving notes handwritten by Serafim, this note reads, "An enquiry esta de Serafim Fortes." Below Serafim's writing, someone else has attempted to make meaning of his Spanglish and has written "ANTIQUITY THIS of Angel." | Photo by Ruby Smith Díaz, City of Vancouver Archives

2

HE ALWAYS FOLLOWED THE SEA

At the tender age of seventeen, Serafim left his family home in Kairi on a ship bound for Liverpool, England.

It's not clear why Serafim decided to leave his home, but there were rumours that he had a quarrel with his family.[4] Maybe in the heat of the moment, Serafim defiantly decided to leave and prove to his family that he could make it on his own, as any teenager might do. Or like I did at age fifteen, when I snuck out of my bedroom window in the dead of night, furious at my mother for not letting me go see my favourite punk bands three and a half hours south of amiskwaciy (Edmonton), so I boarded a Greyhound bus and did it anyway. Or perhaps, as one of the first in his father's family line to be born free, Serafim wanted to experience freedom on open waters, to explore life beyond the island that half of his bloodline was enslaved to.

If indeed this was true, Serafim wouldn't have been the first to dream of life beyond the confines of a plantation. It is estimated that at the beginning of the nineteenth century, one in five out of all sailors on American ships were Black men from either the United States or the Caribbean.[5] Some worked enslaved, and others free. As historian Neil Kennedy describes, seafaring for Black men was "very often a route to freedom, a route to opportunity, a route to masculine expressions of self-worth and roots to communication in the Black Atlantic that were extremely important as well."[6] It is not difficult to imagine that many Black men sought more to life than toiling under the hot, beating sun, carrying out intense physical labour and enduring verbal assaults from plantation owners and human traffickers, day after day. While most white cisgender men across Turtle Island in the mid-nineteenth century also worked physically demanding jobs as farmers, loggers, labourers, and mariners, they enjoyed the freedoms that cisgender Black men didn't—they were able to purchase land almost anywhere they wanted, to purchase homes in any neighbourhood they desired, to vote, to run for government positions, to marry whomever they wanted (so long as it was a heterosexual relationship) without consequence, and, most importantly, to have physical safety.[7]

Although the enslavement of Africans was no longer practised in "British territories" by the time Serafim was a teen, its vestiges still lingered around the world under a different name: capitalism.

Faced with the choice of leading a life bound to a sugar cane or cacao plantation, where he would work endlessly just to fill his hungry belly, or making just enough to survive a voyage in the belly of a ship, traversing the waters into the unknown, Serafim chose the unknown.[8]

Parting at such a young age from the only place he'd ever known was a massive decision and one that required courage and determination. He worked as a cook and deckhand on board, scraping off barnacles, loading cargo, and keeping the ship clean. Within a matter of weeks, Serafim was an entire universe away, making his own way in Liverpool. But his travels didn't end there. He would cross the Atlantic several times on cargo ships, tracing the South American continent and docking in Brasil, Argentina, and back again to Europe. But no matter how hard he worked or how much experience he gained, Serafim's position was never higher than cook or deckhand. As historian Jeff Bolster notes, it was rare for a Black man in the nineteenth century to rise to an officer's berth. Even on international waters with no land in sight, white supremacy reigned.[9]

Finally, after taking in the beauty of the South American coast one more time, Serafim crossed the Atlantic Ocean yet again and decided to settle in Liverpool, England. Liverpool, once known for being a quaint trading town, exploded in size in the early 1800s due to the natural resources stolen abroad by the British Crown. "This massive growth and prosperity was, in the main, paid for by the infamous triangular trade of sugar, tobacco and slaves between the West Indies, Africa and the Americas. Being strategically placed to exploit such transatlantic trade, Liverpool soon became the fastest growing city in the world."[10]

But even in Liverpool, a world away from plantations of sugar cane and coffee trees, Serafim was not fully free. Occupations in England were still limited for Black men, despite the abolition of slavery across the British Empire. He earned a living shining shoes, working as a cook, and taking on odd jobs. Somewhere along the way between Kairi and Liverpool, Serafim took to the water, but this time for his own pleasure—to swim. Oh, to feel his body weightless amid the crushing weight of white supremacy! To leave land and all of its colonial structures behind, diving into the unknown and re-emerging above the current, his lungs affirming his desire to live! Oh, to part water with his own two hands, just like he learned in his Bible book that Moses once did! Maybe between the sweet waters of the River Mersey and his mortal body, Serafim found freedom.

His life-affirming ritual turned many heads, as Europeans were only just beginning to visit rivers and oceans for recreation, and only a handful of individuals had the ability to swim at this time. Sporting competitions between Black people and white people were seen as taboo or were completely outlawed in the United States and much of the Western world, where segregation was used to maintain power over Black communities—especially in the world of sport, where a Black individual could potentially assert their physical superiority over whites, thus threatening the perceived power of white supremacy in society. Despite this, Serafim began competing in local races with young white men from Liverpool, most notably crossing the River Mersey in the dead of night in record time. Although his athletic ability was notable at the time, what was remarkable was his competing against white men. Unbeknownst to him, his skill was a gift that would set him apart years later, on the other side of the world, and for decades to come, until his last breath.

In 1884, after having lived in Liverpool a couple of years, Serafim crossed the ocean waters once again. Perhaps he missed the warm Caribbean sun. Perhaps he didn't feel like he fit in with British society and wanted to be back with his people to eat some buss up, warm curry tones on his tongue, flaky pastry remnants cascading down his chin, cheeks warming. Or maybe as a nineteen-year-old trying to find himself in the world, he simply yearned for more. We will never truly know the reason. The only glimpse we have into his motivations is in an interview with the *Vancouver Daily World*. When asked his reasons for travelling such vast distances, he simply replied that he always followed the sea.[11]

Serafim departed on the *Robert Kerr* from Glasgow, Scotland, joining the crew of Black and white men aboard the transport ship. The *Kerr* was set to travel first to Panamá, bringing supplies for the building of the Panamá Canal, then off to Cape Horn to round the South American continent before finally heading up the Pacific coastline to Victoria in BC, Canada, to restock supplies. Before the completion of the modern-day Panamá Canal, the journey to Victoria was especially arduous and cumbersome for seafarers of the time, lasting over a year if voyaging from Europe.

Serafim's journey aboard the *Robert Kerr* was fraught with life-altering incidents that began shortly after departing Scotland. Serafim and his fellow crewmates were often confined to the bowels of the ship, with no sight of land and no means of communication with the outside world. Only the dull roar of the ship's machinery helped ease their senses enough to find sleep. Waves heaved and sighed for weeks on end, releasing their fury against the sides of the ship, testing the will of the men's minds and bellies to persevere. Sometimes, in absence of the ocean's fury, came the fury of a crew member unleashed upon the tired bodies on board, including Serafim's. I yearned to find out more about Serafim's year at sea. Who were the men he worked alongside? What intrusive thoughts found him in the bowels of that ship, away from any sight of land or humanity? The little that is known about the other men aboard the *Robert Kerr*—names, physical health, abilities, crew positions—survives in a black ruled notebook that was kept by the ship's captain, Edward Edwards. Details such as docking points, destinations, speed, and weather are captured in one or two sentences at most; the myriad experiences of the men on board went mostly undocumented, lost somewhere between strong ocean currents and descriptions of cargo. Of note was the presence of a violent crew member by the name of William C. Anderson, who took every opportunity to verbally and physically assault his shipmates on every leg of the journey.

November 12, 1884
John Richardson, Mate, reported to Captain Edwards, "whilst speaking to Eleazer Riley for muttering whenever he got an order to do anything, William Anderson, AB (able-bodied seaman), called out to Riley, AB, to hit me on the head with something."

November 15, 1884
The ship crossed the Tropic of Capricorn about 550 miles off of Brazil heading south.

December 15, 1884
Ship nearing Cape Horn, off Staten Island (Isla de los Estados).

December 17, 1884
The *Robert Kerr,* at 4:00 p.m., is about 30 miles southeast of the Hermite Islands where Cape Horn is located on Isla Hornos. At 8:00 p.m. the ship was now about 30 miles southeast of the Diego Ramírez Islands and had passed Cape Horn.

December 18, 1884
John Richardson, First Mate, reported to Captain Edwards, "whilst setting the main topsail William Anderson, AB, threatened twice to hit me on the head with a capstan bar."

December 22, 1884
Ship has completed its transit against the strong currents around Cape Horn and was starting to turn north.

December 30, 1884
John Richardson, First Mate, reported to Captain Edwards, "Benjamin Duncan and Emil August, ABs, whilst taking in the mainsail used very abusive language to me and told me I ought to have my head broken."

January 2, 1885
The first mate, John Richardson, reported in the ship's log that: "Seraphim Fortes, AB, came aft and reported that William Anderson, AB, had stuck a cotton hook in his cheek."[12]

The log entry dated January 2, 1885, made my heart stop. "Had stuck a cotton hook in his cheek."

Cheek ripped open. By a white man wielding a cotton hook.

I read the sentence over and over again, a knot forming in my throat.

There were no further notes about the incident. Was it indeed Serafim himself who approached the captain with his bloody cheek to report what had happened? Or did other crewmates report it? And if so, was it the white crewmates who were compelled to bring the incident to the captain's attention and denounce the racist violence on board? Or was it Serafim's

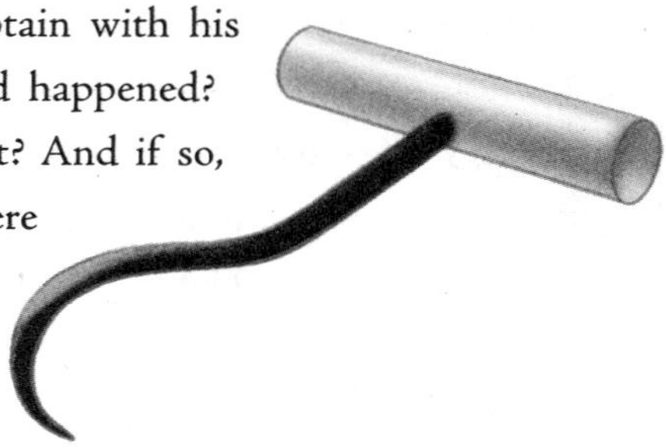

fellow Black crewmates who bravely reported it, despite the threat of retaliation from Anderson?

The next entry on the ship log comes months later and simply states that Serafim became ill for a few days. There are no notes on whether the incident was addressed and how, or on how serious Serafim's wound was. What is clear, however, is that this was a targeted act of racist violence. With a host of tools and weapons available on the ship that Anderson could have used to cause harm, he specifically chose a sharp hook used to process *cotton*. Cotton and its harvest were the backbone of the United States economy, made possible through the enslavement of people of African descent. Using this specific tool to pierce a Black man's cheek was nothing other than a hate crime. It is not difficult to imagine that this violent incident was likely only the tip of the iceberg of racial discrimination experienced by Serafim and other Black men of the ship's crew.

["A Black doctor says the taping by a white surgeon of a noose to a Grande Prairie hospital operating room door in 2016 was a clear threat meant to intimidate him and was part of an escalating pattern of disturbing behaviour that he perceived as racist."[13]*]*

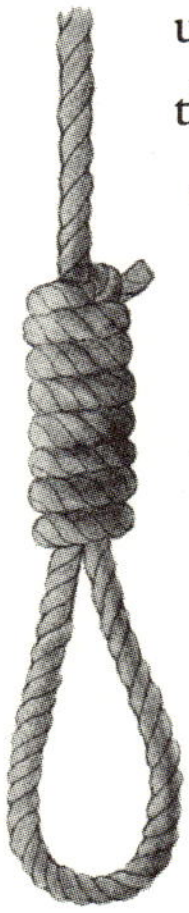

Even if Serafim did bring up the incident again to the captain, it is unlikely the matter would have been taken seriously, considering that the logbook is littered with records of other violent incidents toward other crew members, with seemingly no repercussions for Anderson. Additionally, proving that the incident was anti-Black in nature would have been a futile undertaking, as this sort of behaviour was often excused by Slave Codes across the world.

These Slave Codes first emerged in the former British colony of Barbados in 1661, after a dispute between the naval officer of a human trafficking ship and a human trafficker (plantation owner), wherein the court asserted that "negroes" were "infidels" and, as such, could not become subjects and were therefore alien, to be automatically enslaved and forevermore outside the protection of the law.[14] Furthermore, this legal dispute set a precedent throughout the British colonies that enslaved Africans were "goods" rather than "property."[†] The reverberations of these Slave Codes were still seen throughout British colonies, including in the United States, almost two hundred years later, in the infamous *Dred Scott v. Sandford* ruling. In this case, Dred Scott, a Black man held hostage and enslaved to John Emerson, sued for his freedom. The US Supreme Court declared that Black people "were not, and never could be, American citizens ... and therefore had no right to sue in federal court."[15] With the assertion that Black people were non-human, the state practically sanctioned all forms of violence against Black people at any level of society.

["At a disciplinary hearing ... Wessels denied the noose was meant to be racist or to intimidate or target any person or group."[16]

The College of Physicians and Surgeons of Alberta found him guilty of unprofessional misconduct "but said there was not enough evidence to conclude that Dr. Wynand Wessels 'was motivated by racism or intended to create a racist symbol when he hung the rope on the door.'"[17]*]*

Tragically, violent racist incidents like the one Serafim experienced on the confines of the *Robert Kerr* were not unique, as these ships were often microcosms of white supremacist societies. Sometimes, it was these very microcosms, away from prying eyes and the structures of white supremacy

† Both parties in this court case were arguing for the further dehumanization of enslaved Africans; the case was moreso a matter of semantics, determining whether enslaved Africans were to be considered "goods" or "property." Determining the value of human beings is also intrinsically tied to ableism and ageism, as children, elderly people, and people with disabilities and limbic differences were not considered a whole "good," or pieza, but rather, a half "good," or half pieza. As such, the number of humans involved in this case is counted as between eleven and twenty, depending on how many of the enslaved group of Africans were children, elders, or persons with disabilities or limbic differences.

on land, that lent themselves to the building of relationships across colour lines. As historian Jeff Bolster describes,

> ships could be extraordinarily racist places, and there were many Black men at sea who were subject to horrible invective and insults and beatings by white shipmates. But there were many other instances where Black and white shipmates worked together[,] sailed together, fraternized together, balked at their officers together. And so the best way to put it is that the ship was a workplace in that incredibly racist and slave driven era. The ship was a workplace where Black men sometimes found more freedom or a partial freedom than they would have in a cotton field or tobacco field or working chopping wood for a white person.[18]

[I give gratitude for the lost stories of relationships that sustained long journeys on ocean waters and crossed the colour line, I give gratitude to all those who crossed the seas, with a future predetermined
to grow up and fulfill destiny shining shoes for wealthy whites (and enduring verbal, physical, and/or sexual abuse), or maybe
to grow up and fulfill destiny chopping wood for wealthy whites (and enduring verbal, physical, and/or sexual abuse), or maybe
to grow up and fulfill destiny cooking food for wealthy whites (and enduring verbal, physical, and/or sexual abuse), or maybe
to grow up and take a chance on the water, in the belly of a ship, taking orders from whites (and enduring verbal, physical, and/or sexual abuse, maybe ending up with a hook ripped through their cheek).
I give gratitude to all those who took a chance
on determining their own futures.]

[Below 40 degrees south there is no law. Below 50 degrees south there is no God.[†]*]*

† An old sailing proverb

I imagine what it was like for Serafim to remain aboard the *Robert Kerr*, sharing the same physical space as his assailant, for months on end, perhaps not knowing whether he would survive the voyage. I picture a scared nineteen-year-old, fresh keloid forming on cheek, sailing international waters, months away from land. I picture his thoughts racing, terrified of being further brutalized, not knowing international law but knowing there would be little chance of ever getting justice for someone like him. As I've come to read about Serafim Fortes's life through the eyes of other writers, I am shocked that this violent incident was referenced only once across my research with a couple lines in Lisa Anne Smith and Barbara Rogers's book, *Our Friend Joe*. Even here, however, only a few lines describe the matter, seeming to gloss over the racism embedded in this violent act and the larger anti-Black racism steeped in every aspect of British colonial society.

[Below 40 degrees south there is no law. Below 50 degrees south there is no God.]

The violence didn't end on the *Robert Kerr*,
or on the slave ships,
or on the plantations,
or north of the border,
or in 1800,
or 1900,
or 2018.
It hasn't ended.

Above the fiftieth parallel, I am reminded of the Black Vancouver teen Changich Baboth, who had to sit through homeroom class at Lord Byng Secondary School on Halloween of 2018 with classmates dressed in KKK costumes, while teachers observed this silently. I am reminded of bomb threats directed at Black students in her school that were not taken seriously by administrators because they were "not directed at a specific student" (despite Black students comprising less than 1 percent of the student body at the time).[19]

Above the fortieth parallel, I am reminded of my younger self on a bus in Edmonton on a hot summer's day, making my way home. My brown legs sticking to orange vinyl seats, and my head leaning against the warm windowpane as I breathed in the suffocating dry heat of the prairies. I remember counting the stops until the bus reached the end of *Whyte* Avenue, where it would turn south toward the terminal, just a few blocks from my home. It was here that the words of a young white man at the bus stop flew in through the wide-open window: "Watch the n-----!" The words, in suspended animation, cast a spell of silence among the passengers before finally falling to the gum wrapper–littered floor. In that moment, which lasted a lifetime, the bus lurched forward, leaving a part of me and my thoughts behind at that bus stop on Whyte Avenue.

[Below 40 degrees south there is no law. Below 50 degrees south there is no God.]

Though over a hundred years have lapsed since Serafim's passing, feelings of isolation and fear caused by white supremacist violence on Black communities on Turtle Island remain the same.

[you were not made of cotton
nor was your tongue meant to taste blood
no, you were shaped in the likeness of Ochosí,
Protector of life and justice
with a spine never yielding
to the weight of bigotry
and hands strong enough
to break the cusp of ocean wave,
to ask for its medicine,
to rinse seared flesh

while resisting the bitter sting
of swallowing pride.

no, you were not made of cotton
nor was your heart made to become steel
no, you were human
not made for instruments to pierce
not impermeable to insults
or threats of death

no, you were not made of cotton
not made to be punctured
not made to be maimed
not meant to be left to bleed upon a ship deck
in an aimless vessel
suspended in space and time
with no witness]

The *Robert Kerr* sailed on. Changich survived. Serafim survived, and so did I.

And so too will many after us.

Many more notes were made in the logbook in the months after about the ongoing "trouble" created by Anderson on the *Robert Kerr,* including his hitting crew members with a metal bar and other crew members fearing for their lives. While there is no further information about the motives for the attacks or the ethnicities of the victims, it is evident that Anderson was a violent man. Echoes of his brutality would have reverberated in every corner of the *Robert Kerr,* leaving no person untouched.

Unbeknownst to the crew, the looming violence onboard was just a premonition of the ship's cursed destiny in the months to come.

3

ALL CRAB FIND DEY HOLE

Months after Serafim was violently assaulted, the ship's captain, Edward Edwards, took ill. Various rudimentary attempts were made by ship hands to aid his ailing health; however, none were successful, and Captain Edwards eventually succumbed to his illness at sea.

Left without a captain, the crew pushed on, undeterred. But once again, fate was not on their side. On September 6, 1885, the vessel's forefront and keel were severely damaged during a storm off the coast of San Juan Island. Within a period of twenty-four hours, the *Robert Kerr* was towed from San Juan Island to Active Pass and finally to the township of Granville, which would later come to be known as Vancouver.

Here, in one of the inner harbours, the ship's crew worked tirelessly for seventeen days to pump water out of the ship. Serafim's body reached its breaking point, and he was placed on the sick list while the rest of the crew did their best to salvage the sinking ship. But it was no use. The next day, the *Robert Kerr* was condemned.

And so, thousands of miles away from the places that the men called home, the crew of eighteen was discharged.[20] Serafim decided to try his luck on the territories of the xʷməθkʷəy̓əm (Musqueam), Sk̲wx̱wú7mesh (Squamish), and səlilwətaɬ (Tsleil-Waututh) Nations. He was about twenty years old at this time. He would never return to Trinidad.

Canada was not dissimilar to Trinidad. It too was a British colony that utilized the theft of Indigenous lands and the enslavement of Black people to amass significant amounts of wealth and advance the settler colonial project.† Early colonizer accounts speak to the thriving ecosystems, pristine waters, and abundance of fresh air all across Turtle Island. The lands, so well cared for by Indigenous nations for thousands of years, appeared to be untouched—further bolstering the idea of terra nullius, the concept that "empty" land can be acquired by occupation. This concept, critical to settler colonialism, was based on the colonial mentality of property ownership being strictly defined by visible and permanent infrastructure on land, with permanent residences in singular confined areas, altered and manicured ecosystems, and a "civilized" white population. For Europeans coming from vastly polluted and devastated lands in the thick of the Industrial Revolution and the Scramble for Africa, Turtle Island represented one final opportunity for wealth and conquest.

But does a nation need to be *seen* by a European or a settler colonial state in order to exist? Canada argued yes, as in the case of the Lubicon Nation of Northern Alberta, who were "missed" in treaty signings and are therefore not entitled to Aboriginal rights and title to this day, though they do very much exist. Canada also argued that a nation must be seen by Europeans in order to exist in the case of the Sinixt Nation in the Interior of British Columbia, who were declared "extinct" in 1956 by the federal government even though numerous people of the Nation are very much alive to this day.[21] It took sixty-five years for the claim to be overturned by the Supreme Court in 2021. The term *terra nullius* is complicated by the very concept of visibility, begging the question: visible from where and by whom?

In the case of early British explorer Captain George Vancouver, much of the land that came to be known as Vancouver was designated as terra nullius because he didn't bother to check whether any people were inhabiting the spaces beyond the water's edge, despite there being defined and permanent infrastructure on the land. As Chief August Jack Khatsahlano

† Treaties were signed under duress, and a significant portion of Canada has never been surrendered through treaty or war.

of the Squamish Nation explained in conversation with James Skitt Matthews, the city's first official archivist,†

> Vancouver reports that when, in 1792, he passed through our First Narrows, he saw no signs of habitations; yet actually there were two large villages close at hand; one at Homulchesan (Capilano) and the other at Whoi-Whoi (Lumberman's Arch, Stanley Park). The explanation most likely is that, following their usual customs, these two villages were slightly back from their beaches, and hidden from the sight of passersby, for one authority, Chief Matthias Joe, states positively that until the white men guaranteed safety, Indian villages were concealed thus in the trees, to hide them from the sight of possible foes.[22]

On a geographic level, Vancouver moved through a rapid sequence of monumental changes at the turn of the twentieth century. At the root of it all was the clearing of land and the violent displacement of xʷməθkʷəy̓əm, Sḵwx̱wú7mesh, and səlilwətaɬ Nations from their lands onto small parcels of racially segregated land called reserves. This forced displacement allowed logging to become the primary industry driving economic growth for white settlers, and it later drew communities of Chinese, Japanese, Portuguese, and South Asian origin to take part in the booming industry. Towering old-growth landscapes and ecosystems were destroyed. Longhouses and sacred sites were cleared. The fledgling township of Vancouver was permanently shrouded by a thick layer of smoke, due to the constant clearing and burning of shrubbery and limb-stripped trees. Between 1900 and 1910, the population more than quadrupled from 26,000 to 120,000, with settlers appropriating land for themselves across the Lower Mainland.

† "Official" as in formally recognized by the city for archiving documents and photographs. Archivists have always existed on these lands, but under different names, such as knowledge keepers, song keepers, Elders, and more. These roles and titles are rarely, if ever, recognized by municipal or provincial institutions.

A view of English Bay from below the Beach Avenue entrance to Stanley Park, showing the entrance to False Creek, the Kitsilano Indian Reserve (Seṅák̲w), and Fairview. | W.T. Dalton, City of Vancouver Archives, AM54-S4-1-L-12-: L-12-37

Despite the widespread acceptance of terra nullius among settlers, the ability to own or occupy stolen land was not equally accessible to all settler communities. The segregation tenets of many neighbourhoods across so-called British Columbia banned non-whites from owning homes or living in white neighbourhoods during this time. As one discriminatory covenant from a South Vancouver land title still reads to this day, "No Asiatic, Negro, or Indian shall have the right or be allowed to own, become tenant of, or occupy any part of [the property]."[23] Other communities such as the "British Properties" in West Vancouver had similar segregation policies. These covenants helped solidify the push for non-white communities to form their own enclaves out of necessity, solidarity, love, and survival. As a result, communities such as Chinatown, Paueru Gai (Japantown), and Hogan's Alley also began to take shape in Vancouver at the turn of the century, with some communities lasting into the 1960s and present-day Vancouver.[†]

† Hogan's Alley rose to prominence in Vancouver in the 1930s and was a place where many racialized groups established their homes. This neighbourhood was also the heart of Vancouver's Black community until it was destroyed by the City of Vancouver in 1967.

Seraphim standing in front of his tent at Íýelshn. | City of Vancouver Archives AM54-s4--Port P1725

Young Serafim was no exception to participating in this land grab. In fact, in an early account, Serafim claimed to have proudly "discovered" Íỷeḻshn one day while paddling along the inlet shore, making no mention of the Squamish Nation or the cultural significance of that land.[24] If he was aware of whose territory Íỷeḻshn belonged to, he chose to ignore it, and he established his home on what he viewed as empty land.

As Smith and Rogers describe in *Our Friend Joe*,

> at some unrecorded point in the early days of his city employee status, Joe took up residence in a canvas tent at the southeast corner of Davie and Denman streets. He was joining beachgoers who for several years had been helping themselves to small parcels of English Bay waterfront. A ragtag assortment of tents, driftwood lean-tos and rudimentary shacks lined the shore. Joe's tent stood atop a wooden platform, ensuring a floor that was high and dry on rainy days.[25]

Once again, the place where Serafim set himself up in was *not* "empty." In an interview from 1951, recounting the colonial history of English Bay, James Skitt Matthews said,

> ninety years ago [1840]—all Vancouver was hidden beneath a dense forest towering 250 feet to the skies. Along the shores where we are now sitting the waters, at high tide, lapped the lower branches and, again, this beach was covered with large and small boulders, the remains of which you see on my right. These boulders were covered with sharp mussel shells which cut the bare feet. They have long since been removed. Now, there were three to five thousand Indians living on English Bay. They were canoe Indians—their home was the sea and the shore.[26]

In other times, a land grab as enacted by non-Indigenous people in the nineteenth and twentieth centuries would have been inconceivable to the three nations who have lived since time immemorial in and around

Vancouver.[†] As Sundance Chief Rueben George of the səlilwətaɬ Nation explained, "Our people always had to wait in our canoes before coming onto another nation's shore. We had to ask for permission to come onto someone else's land. Coming out of the canoe and onto another nation's shore without consent was considered an act of war."[27]

Permission to use land was rarely, if ever, sought by settlers of the era. However, smallpox brought by settlers devastated Indigenous communities—the səlilwətaɬ Nation was decimated from ten thousand strong to just eleven people—eroding their capacity to present a physical force to assert traditional laws and territorial boundaries.[28] In addition, the federal government's systematic kidnapping of Indigenous children, facilitated through the Indian Act of 1876 but beginning in some places as early as 1831, further undermined the Nation's capacity to defend their village sites and seasonal camps.[29] Íýelshn was one of those seasonal camps used by the Squamish Nation, with archeological evidence of this tracing back to ten thousand years ago. In the face of systemic violence aimed at eradicating Indigenous peoples and ways of life, Íýelshn was completely usurped by squatters/settlers and then renamed to English Bay, the name that is used to this day.

It is difficult to fully grasp the ecological destruction and colonial violence that took place during this time.

I find myself at the foot of second-growth cedar stumps, surrounded by steel and glass giants, moved to tears as I mourn this land's devastation. I trace my fingers along the gashes created as footholds from which to topple thousands of years of history. I imagine what it would it have been like to live in a place where the trees dwarf me and to trace my way around their bases, walking metre upon metre before encountering my own footsteps in the soft earth again. I find myself exasperated by the desire of settler colonial society to insatiably destroy raw beauty, claim land, and then claim everything that grew out of it as a prize. [*"No one*

† And still to this present day

would ever dream that, during the salmon run, English Bay would be so full of fish one could figuratively, almost cross to the south shore by stepping from fish to fish, and still harder to believe that I caught a salmon at the corner of Maple Street and Third Avenue."[30]]

I am filled with deep sorrow, knowing that these lands were once so bountiful that settlers thought no matter how much they took, it would never run out. I wonder what it would have been like to stand at the shores of Íy̓el̓shn and hear whispers of the "West End" forest, and only be able to reach X̱wáy̓x̱way (Stanley Park) through small trails thick with salal. I walk and wonder what it was like to live at the turn of the century. I cannot begin to fathom the enormity of the ever-present grief Indigenous peoples must walk with, seeing the lands their ancestors have been on since time immemorial turn to ash and be fenced up as private property.

[Then they grow away from the Earth
then they grow away from the sun
then they grow away from the plants and
animals.
They see no life
When they look
they only see objects.
The world is a dead thing for them
the trees and rivers are not alive
the mountains and stones are not alive.[31]]

At the time of Serafim's arrival in Vancouver in 1885, only fifty-one years had lapsed since the abolition of slavery across the British Empire. The economic and social systems that relied on white supremacy and anti-Black racism would linger for many more generations to come. In 1885, a white settler in their seventies would have lived through their formative teenage years with the enslavement and dehumanization of Black communities as the status quo of the British Empire. Younger generations would have gradually begun to see the slow dismantling of slavery throughout their lifetimes, and only one or two generations would have experienced their country as being completely free of it.

As historian James W. St.G. Walker asserts, "Black enslavement made a powerful impression on whites ... it was impossible to witness the transfer of status from a legal condition to a biological characteristic, from 'slave' to 'black.'"[32†] Therefore, the imprint left by a history of slavery on the Canadian psyche is impossible to ignore when placing Serafim within the twentieth-century context. *Slave* and *Black*, or *slave* and *Negro*, were practically synonymous. Even today, many authors use the word *slaves* to describe people of African descent who were victims of human trafficking, without distinguishing the human beings from the ways in which they were held in bondage, or from the people responsible for their enslavement, trafficking, and genocide. There is no doubt that these imprints on the white settler psyche that are alive today were also strongly present when Serafim and other Black settlers and refugees arrived in Vancouver.

As a society firmly entrenched in racial segregation, Serafim's labour options were limited to bootblack, porter, cook, bartender, or an odd-jobs man—all among the lowest-paying jobs. He tried nearly all of them before settling into bartending at the newly built luxurious Alhambra Hotel. The Alhambra was built in the Victorian-Italianate style at the water's edge and boasted a fireplace in every room. This area it was built in later became known as Gastown, named after a white pedophile by the name of John "Gassy Jack" Deighton. Deighton was a gold prospector, seaman, and riverboat pilot who, at the age of forty, "married" a twelve-year-old Indigenous girl by the name of Kwa7xiliya from the Squamish Nation. Kwa7xiliya ran away shortly after giving birth to their son. (In the 1970s,

† This "powerful impression" has lingered into the present day, as evidenced by the fact that Black communities in Canada have, on average, the lowest income across the country and are the most likely to be targeted by carding practices. (Carding refers to the police practice of arbitrarily stopping individuals and documenting their personal information.) Black communities are also one of the most overrepresented racial groups in Canadian prisons and the most likely to be killed in police-involved interactions.

a statue honouring Deighton was erected in Gastown, where it stood until 2022, when it was toppled by protesters.[33])

It was here, in the heart of the new settler colonial project, that Serafim served drinks to loggers, seamen, and American prospectors on their way to try their luck in the hunt for gold up the West Coast. It was here that Serafim gained notoriety as a man of God for being able to maintain an orderly environment among intoxicated and aggressive men, who were known to prey upon young Indigenous women and girls.

Even while working at the Alhambra Hotel, Serafim attended church every Sunday and continued to spend time in the water by Íỷel̓shn's shores. It didn't take too long for other squatters to take note of his exceptional strength and power in the water. As more land was snatched up and more smoke filled the skies from burn piles of brush and branches in the aftermath of logging, more settlers came to the water to find reprieve for their lungs. Íỷel̓shn became a prime destination, with its sandy beach and close proximity to the newly emerging downtown core. Soon, swaths of Vancouverites made a habit of heading to the water to unwind and to gather, despite not knowing how to swim.

While it is unclear whether there were official policies about segregation at Íỷel̓shn, it is not a far stretch to assume that there were. In a city document, social scientist Leonard Marsh noted that the presence of Black families outside of Hogan's Alley was unwelcome.[34] Crystal Pool, built seven years after Serafim's death, a mere 2.2 kilometres from English Bay, was formally segregated until 1945. Sometime within these years, "Brown Skin Beach," which was located on Sen̓áḵw (the winter camp for the Squamish Nat̨ion), was rumoured to have come into prominence for the Black community in response to their not being able to access other beaches in the city.[35] Though it is unclear how popular this beach was or whether Indigenous peoples or other racialized groups shared the space, it is evident that Black people did not have access to public spaces in the same way that whites did. Perhaps Serafim's presence on English Bay Beach was tolerated by white settler society as a literal matter of life or death—settlers and their children needed him present in order to enjoy the beach without drowning. Within this contradiction, Serafim's critical skill set and consistent presence at Íỷeḯshn transformed him into a celebrity, a solitary Black man in a time and place where segregation was active and physical proximity to and contact with Black people was both taboo and a means to elevate the class status of white families.

With every passing year, Serafim's presence at Íỷeḯshn came to be expected by white settlers. Alongside the growing expectation of his servitude, his role expanded to swim instructor, trash collector, and special constable of the Vancouver Police Department by 1900—all with no pay.

But, as with any other period of history, there were some within the dominant group who broke away from the norm and demanded change in 1901. Many Vancouverites living in occupied Íỷeḯshn saw Serafim's unpaid service as unacceptable and began to take action, first by circulating petitions that had all signees contribute a small amount of money on a monthly basis for a total of three months, with the hopes that the City of Vancouver would then take over and provide him with a salary. Many also sent letters to newspaper editors, praising Serafim for his invaluable service and demanding he be compensated for his labour. Finally, city council begrudgingly took the issue to a council meeting. Thomas Neelander attempted to thwart the decision to pay Serafim, calling him a "lazy oaf," warning that providing him with a salary would set a bad precedent, and claiming that he had misused his special constable powers on multiple occasions.[36] Despite Neelander's efforts, the city made Serafim an employee, paying him a mere eighty dollars a month for live-in, on-call services.

> When it was presented to City Council it had garnered thousands of signatures. Council immediately agreed, appointing Joe swimming instructor, lifeguard and special constable of English Bay with a salary of $80.00 a month, a not insignificant sum at the time. Characteristically,

> the mayor and councillors came down to the beach and had to call Joe out of the water to tell him the good news.[37]

Under the new salary, Serafim's responsibilities encapsulated all of his previous unpaid work. Under his title of special constable of the Vancouver Police Department, he could enforce orderly conduct at English Bay, for which he was allowed to carry a revolver.[38] It is important to note that this title appears to not have held any real power; special constables are limited in scope and authority, and the Vancouver Police Department asserts that Arthur Bruce Clarke was in fact the first Black man hired to the force in 1969, after decades of not finding any "suitable" Black candidates to join. Clarke speaks of having been denied promotions and having to "work harder than everyone else" to receive equal treatment.[39] Even fifty years after Serafim's death, the struggle with anti-Black racism within the police force continued. It is not difficult to imagine that, although Serafim seemed to be proud at times of his special constable designation, the racism in the police force then would have been similar to or worse than the level of racism in the force in 1969 and today.

In 1910, the City of Vancouver officially recognized Serafim as the English Bay lifeguard. While this gesture initially appears to be a commendable one, it is crucial to highlight the context that created the situation of Serafim's being unpaid for many years and living in poverty. As in many cities around the world, there were but a few segregated, poorly paid occupations that Black people were permitted to hold. This ensured that whites always held more power over non-whites and that it was difficult, if not impossible, for non-whites to amass any kind of wealth. Given the stereotypes at the time that equated Blackness with laziness and stupidity, Serafim *had* to be an extraordinarily industrious man with some proximity to whites in order for white citizens to take notice of him and be moved to take action to improve his living conditions.

But what did it mean for Serafim to have the role of special constable in a white supremacist settler society? What did it mean for him to hold a position of authority on a likely segregated beach? What did it mean for a Black man to help himself to land on Íýelshn's shores?

With his eighty-dollar salary, Serafim continued living in a canvas tent surrounded by salal and tall cedars until 1905, when he petitioned the City of Vancouver to allow him to take over the former cabin of a settler family just steps away from the water's edge. This cabin would allow him to be a caretaker of Íýelshn all year round, from the comfort of four walls and a solid roof. There, he would remain until the end of his life, providing lifeguarding services not only at the shoreline, but also as far east as X̱áywá7esks (False Creek) and as far south as X̱ats'alanexw (Kitsilano). His cabin was sheltered by six elm trees that provided a quiet and smoke-free refuge from the bustling new city. Across the water was Seńáḵw. But in 1913, Serafim's view over the inlet changed forever when British Columbia Conservative Premier Richard McBride forcibly removed all Squamish people from Seńáḵw to make room for the growing city.[40] The process was an especially violent one.

As Khelsilem Rivers of the Squamish Nation describes,

> in 1911 there were eleven families living there, government authorities came in and they told those eleven families: "We're going to give you some cash. You have to get on this barge and we're going to ship you out and we're buying the land from you. And if you don't leave, we're going to forcibly move you, or kill you."[41]

It is difficult to even begin to fathom the horrific trauma experienced by the Squamish Nation at this time, being forced at gunpoint to give up their ancestral village site and their homes, get onto a barge meant for cargo, and be transported to X̱wemelch'stn, the present-day Capilano Reserve under the Lions Gate Bridge. It is equally difficult to imagine that Serafim wouldn't have noticed such a life-altering event, happening in plain sight of his cabin, that left an entire coastline empty. Although I haven't come across any literature that specifically describes a relationship between Serafim and members of the Squamish Nation, I believe he would have interacted with Squamish people coming to shore to fish, hunt, and gather medicines, as they had for thousands of years.

Whether Serafim would have connected the displacement of the Squamish Nation with the larger settler colonial project is hard to say. The Canadian propaganda machine at this time[†] relied heavily on perpetuating the terra nullius narrative and manifested it through the reserve system, clearing Indigenous communities and thousands of years of ancestral connection to their lands and displacing them away from settler colonial townships and urban centres—away from proximity to whites—thus propagating the settler myth that the lands were "empty" before the arrival of whites. To this day, the terra nullius fantasy holds so strong over settlers and refugees that many are shocked to learn the land they are living on in Canada had been inhabited for at least ten thousand years prior to the arrival of settlers.

While I like to imagine that Serafim, as a Black man from Trinidad, was acutely attuned to racism and violence within the settler colonial process and empathized with the plight of the Squamish Nation, it is not necessarily a historically accurate imagining of how he understood his positionality within Vancouver. In fact, Serafim seemed to have felt quite comfortable within settler colonial society and within his role as special constable on a likely segregated, predominantly white beach, going so far as to abuse his authority multiple times against Chinese communities.

Serafim would likely have bought into the settler colonial narrative, partly as a matter of survival and partly as a matter of self-interest and comfort, as do many migrants to this day. In the end, he might have considered himself to be just another person among the many helping

† And to the present day

View of Kitsilano Indian Reserve (Seṅáḵw), looking east. In the canoe are Chief August Jack Khatsahlano and his wife and child. | W. Chapman, City of Vancouver Archives AM1376-: CVA 1376-203

themselves to land, elevating their socio-economic status, and assuring a future for themselves in the process, no matter the cost.[†]

[So the other witches said
"Okay you win; you take the prize,
but what you just said just now -
it isn't so funny
It doesn't sound so good.
We are doing okay without that kind of thing
Take it back.
Call that story back."

But the witch just shook its head
at the others in their stinking animal skins, fur
and feathers.
It's already turned loose.
It's already coming.
It can't be called back.[42]]

† A part of me deeply mourns this realization. I have to separate my deep desire for decolonization across the globe and for solidarity among all people of African descent in dismantling the structures that enslaved us and profited off our lands, our bodies, and the stolen lands and bodies of other Indigenous nations across the world from the reality that the Black experience is not a monolith. Many individuals, throughout history and still now, seek wealth, self-aggrandizing opportunities, and power above all else, no matter the cost. The Maroons of Jamaica, from my ancestral homelands, fought for the liberation of enslaved Africans and forced the British to sign the first treaty in the Caribbean; they accepted terms in that treaty to return escaped enslaved kin back to the plantation owners and human traffickers they escaped from. Although I will never understand such betrayals, these are the contradictions I must reckon with, if I am to write truthfully.

4 READING BETWEEN THE LINES OF WHITE SUPREMACY

> To live in the Black Diaspora is I think to live as a fiction—a creation of empires, and also self-creation. It is to be a being living inside and outside of herself.
>
> —DIONNE BRAND

As an Afro Latina person, conducting research on Serafim Fortes's life wasn't only about finding out his accomplishments or the dates on which they occurred. It was also learning about the historical context in which he lived in order to disentangle who he really was from what the white gaze wanted him to be. I had to constantly read between the lines of what was being reported, constantly skirt around racist and condescending language in articles that intended to praise Serafim and his accomplishments. I quickly realized that to research his life, I needed to contort my language to match the language of white journalists and archivists of the time and utilize out-of-date terms such as *Negroes* and *Negroes of Vancouver* so that I could locate more substantial information on Black communities. Even then, the information I found was scarce—a testament to the heartbreaking truth that most often, the figures we know about today and see in a positive light are those whom the dominant society deemed worthy of archiving. I'm not the only one who has encountered barriers when searching for Black histories in the archives.

Black curator Nya Lewis asserts that racism in archival work in Vancouver has negatively impacted the preservation of Black histories and legacies. Through their recovery of Black communities' photos, predominantly in police records, and their work connecting with Black communities for their own personal photography collections, Lewis is able to challenge "the insufficient depository of knowledge contributing to the historical trajectory of restricting representations of Blackness to caricature, ethnographic object, or criminal."[43] It is incredibly telling about the state of overcriminalization in Canada that one has to resort to searching the police archives for evidence of Black communities' existence. For me, researching Serafim's life has highlighted this insufficient depository of knowledge. So, I tasked myself with reimagining his life not as a caricature, ethnographic object, or criminal, but rather as an uncle I never knew.

The way in which Serafim was often written about by early-twentieth-century white settlers was vastly shaped by racist minstrel representations of African American people drawn in cartoon style with wide smiles; exaggerated large noses; thick, oversized bright-red lips; and skin in a uniform matte-black ink. African American characters were depicted as simple minded, unintelligent, uneducated, asexual, desireless, subservient, and always a source of laughter and entertainment for the white American viewer. Their accents were often of the Southern United States and littered with grammatical errors so as to suggest a lower-class status and lack of education. African Estadounidenses* were almost always depicted in the domain they were enslaved to: the cotton field, the "master's" house, or a rundown shack.†

† *Estadounidenses* is a Spanish word meaning "citizen of the United States." This word does not exist in English, highlighting the fact that the United States exercises passive hegemony on a global scale, even in something as basic as language. The word *America* should refer collectively North, Central, and South America rather than being assigned by default to a single country in the Americas. To continue this naming practice erases the presence of all other countries in the three continents, particularly those in the Global South. I also use an asterisk after Estadounidenses to reflect that enslaved Africans and persons of African descent were not considered human beings or citizens of the United States of America until 1868. This dehumanization survives still through lack of reparations and systemic anti-Black racism, including the disproportionate killing of Black people, the incarceration (and re-enslavement) of Black people, and stand-your-ground laws that allow the use of deadly force with little to no consequence for the shooter.

This minstrel flattening of the African diaspora carried through north of the border, despite Canada having had a different historical context for individuals of African descent living within the country. No human trafficking ships came directly to Canada, so early Black presence here often signalled human trafficking activity by French, British, and US settlers in the eastern provinces of modern-day Quebec, Ontario, Nova Scotia, and Prince Edward Island. Due to the colder northern climate, the enslavement of Black individuals was based predominantly in domestic work within the homes of affluent whites, rather than the large-scale plantation-based enslavement as seen throughout Latin America, the Caribbean, and the United States. Despite the drastically different histories and geographies of Canada and the United States, racist stereotypes rooted in US plantation–style slavery still prevailed in Canada and were applied to Black individuals like Serafim Fortes.

After the "American Revolutionary War" and the War of 1812, many Black Loyalists arrived in Canada. These were enslaved Black individuals in the United States who had fought for the British, having been promised land and freedom in Canada. Some soon found out that the stolen land they had been given was rocky and not suitable for cultivation, while others found out that not only would they not receive any land, but they also faced violent racist threats for living adjacent to white communities. In so-called Nova Scotia, Mi'kmaq people often took in runaway and formerly enslaved Black individuals as kin, teaching them how to survive harsh winters and making a home for them within Mi'kmaq communities.

Black communities in early Canada held varying degrees of freedom, even after 1834, when slavery was supposedly abolished in the British colonies. Abolition did not immediately translate to emancipation for formerly enslaved Black peoples. Instead, they were forced into transitional roles as unpaid "apprentices" for an additional seven years, for the profit and benefit of the human trafficker to whom they "belonged." In addition, post-emancipation, the British government compensated human traffickers / slave owners for their "loss of property," to the tune of twenty million pounds, whereas the formerly enslaved people received nothing. To make matters worse, formerly enslaved people were often forced into squalor due to the systemic racism that limited them from most occupations that paid higher wages. Whites sometimes even rioted against Black people's attaining any kind of wage at all for their labour, as in the 1784 riots in Shelburne, Nova Scotia.

Following the 1834 "abolition" of slavery in the British colonies, another wave of migration arose, with many Black individuals attempting to flee the United States for Canada to find land, safety, and some form of refuge. However, the passing of the 1850 Fugitive Slave Act in the United States required that any person of African descent who had escaped their bondage be returned to the human trafficker who had held them captive, which triggered another wave of migration across the border. Once again, Canada proved not to be a safe haven, as many white settlers actively sought out Black refugees and recaptured them to return them across the border. They also targeted Black individuals living in Canada who were born free or had been recently freed through the Abolition Act.

It was within this context of hypersurveillance that Serafim arrived in Canada, from one British colony to another—emancipated, but not free.†

In British Columbia, the majority of early Black migration occurred through the invitation of Governor James Douglas in 1858. Douglas, a man of Scottish and Barbadian-Creole ancestry, extended an invitation to Black communities in California to settle on the newly stolen Vancouver Island colony. Approximately eight hundred African Estadounidenses* took him up on this invitation as a chance to escape growing white supremacist violence and the threat of being re-enslaved through changing California

† A nod to Rinaldo Walcott's *The Long Emancipation: Moving Toward Black Freedom*, which defines *freedom* as something that is yet to be experienced by Black people and that must exist outside of the legal framework connected to enslavement. Currently, we are in the process of the "long emancipation," which has been in process since the "abolition" of chattel slavery on Turtle Island. Many systemic vestiges of enslavement exist in Canada and the United States, most visibly in the overrepresentation of Black individuals in the criminal (in)justice system and the disproportionate number of Black fatalities in police interactions across Canada, reminding us yet again that we are in the process of emancipation, but we are not free.

state laws. Douglas offered Black communities stolen land in Victoria, but the majority of Black families ended up settling on the W̱SÁNEĆ, Quw'utsun, and Stz'uminus territories, colonially known as Salt Spring Island. Most families eventually moved back to California in the years after the American Civil War.

Despite Douglas's ancestry, his intentions cannot be solely seen as a compassionate gesture toward Black communities. As a colonial governor, Douglas was acutely aware of the threat to his colonial aspirations for the newly stolen territory posed by US citizens travelling up the British Columbia coast in search of gold. These aspirations relied on the theft of Indigenous lands and also required the suppression of Indigenous resistance through colonial policy and war.[†]

Despite this migration by African Estadounidenses* to so-called British Columbia, the overall number of Black individuals in Vancouver remained small at the turn of the century. The 1891 Vancouver Census cites only twenty-seven Black individuals living in Vancouver, half of whom were from the same two families. There were no large migration waves of Black communities of Caribbean origin until after World War II, through the West Indian Domestic Scheme.[‡] It is highly likely, therefore, that Serafim was the only person of Caribbean descent living in Vancouver between his arrival in 1885 until his death in 1922. As unique as this experience would have been, his experience as an Afro Latino man of Caribbean origin made his identity even more distinctive.

To the rest of white settler society, however, Serafim was likely just Black. With such a small population of Black individuals among a predominantly white settler population, white settlers easily reduced Serafim

† As demonstrated by the sending out of gunboats in response to the murder of three white sailors who were attempting to trespass on Kwakwa̱ka̱'wakw territory, as well as the sending out of a royal gunboat to Salt Spring Island to ward off Indigenous nations after Black settlers complained of being threatened by Indigenous people who continued using their own lands, which had been taken from them by force and "given" to Black communities from California.

‡ This immigration program brought approximately three thousand West Indian women to work in Canada as "domestics" in affluent households. See https://www.canada.ca/en/parks-canada/news/2020/07/west-indian-domestic-scheme-19551967.html.

Serafim in front of the boulder on English Bay Beach. | City of Vancouver Archives AM54-S4-: Port P1775

to an "American" minstrel caricature. In many interviews, reporters approximated a Black Southern accent for Serafim by including phonetic spellings of common words, such as "hyar you," "keep outside dar," and "kick yo feet, chile, kick yo feet." Serafim, who was never documented to have stepped foot in the Southern United States, could never have developed a Southern accent. If anything, his English would have been shaped by the cadence of Spanish and Patois—the native tongues he grew up with in Trinidad—and perhaps some British influence from his two-year stay in Liverpool. Eventually, after living in Canada for decades, he likely didn't have very much of a "foreign" accent at all. The white minstrel fantasy went further than speech patterns, however, as evidenced by multiple newspaper articles highlighting Serafim's "eagerness to please," further ingraining the trope of the Southern Black slave.

In stark contrast, the account of Goldvine Howard does not include these speech inflections when quoting Serafim. Goldvine Howard was the daughter of Samuel Howard and Catherine "Cassie" Howard (née Scurry). Her grandparents were African Estadounidenses* migrants Martha and Hiram Scurry, and they ran a rooming house as well as a barbershop in downtown Vancouver. The rooming house provided Serafim with seasonal shelter for many years, and as a result, a tight bond was formed between Serafim and the Scurry family.[44] When Goldvine described Serafim teaching her how to swim, she simply quoted him as saying, "Kick your feet. No, I won't let you go. Kick your feet."[45] At no point did she mention an accent or give any indication that Serafim's speech pattern was any different from hers. Her reflections as a Black woman and a close family friend give us perhaps the most accurate insight into how Serafim really spoke and break the fantasy of Serafim as a Southern Negro.

Historical documents about Serafim's early life are sparse, and his own writing, rumoured to be an autobiography, has never been found. Over a century has lapsed since his death, and sparse historical documents are all we have to glean details from. His identity as a Trinidadian-born Afro Latino man is what made him the man whom Vancouverites came to know and love. But for the most part, his Caribbean identity and all the cultures within it—the foundation of his life—have not been given much consideration in the accounts that have been written. I argue that it has been difficult, if not impossible, for the non-Black people who have written about his life to accurately reflect all the aspects of Serafim's life.

For me, as an Afro Latina, my roots are intertwined with my identity. My roots shape how I see the world. My roots allow me to reclaim my own narrative when it is seized by the gaze of the other. Even as an Afro Latina, my identity has always been constantly scrutinized by white Latine people in Canada. I can't recall being immediately addressed in Spanish at any Latine event that I've gone to. Instead, it is almost always assumed that I speak only English, despite Latin America and the Caribbean having the largest concentration of people of African descent outside of Africa due to the transatlantic slave trade.[46]

As a child, I recall peñas that I would look forward to attending all year round—being able to eat empanadas and listen the sounds of the charango, zampoña, and tambor in the company of my community was like a dream come true. At the same time, the experiences became incredibly dissociative for me; my mom would be asked if I was adopted or "¿La niña habla Español?" while I was standing right beside her. Jumping to the challenge, I would introduce myself in Spanish and speak as clearly and articulately as I could, determined to impress the other Latines who were questioning my identity. Every single time, they were amazed, and often, I would be led around the room to meet others and demonstrate my Spanish *["y sí, tiene acento chileno también"]*. As a young child I would feel proud, seeing how pleased my mom was when I captivated the other Chileans in the room, knowing that other Latine kids born and raised in Canada could not speak as proficiently as me because their parents had told them to speak only English at home in hopes of assimilating to have a better life. But as I grew older, I found the experience of being led around the room to be anxiety inducing; I felt I *had* to prove my mastery in Spanish in order to be truly accepted as a Latina. It is only as an adult that I have been able to learn and understand that the only reason I ever had to prove myself was to rise above the scrutiny of the white supremacist gaze.

[I will not be crunched into other people's fantasies and eaten alive.†]

In my schooling experience in amiskwaciy, I was almost always the only Black student in class and one of a handful of Black students in the entire school. Most of the other students were white and of Polish or Ukrainian descent. To my gym teachers' dismay, I failed miserably at basketball and track, crushing their dreams of me embodying the Black athlete stereotype.

To make matters worse, I wasn't thin, I couldn't afford the trendiest clothes, and I wore glasses, making me seriously uncool. So, in junior high, when other students excitedly found out that I had Jamaican lineage, I saw my opportunity to rise above my plight. "Of course my dad smokes marijuana all the time. Of course my dad wears Rasta hats. Of course I have every single Bob Marley album." None of it was true. But I leaned into it. I left my Chilean identity behind. It was finally my chance to be cool. It failed.

[I will not be crunched into other people's fantasies and eaten alive.]

And so, I imagine Serafim's experience through my own stories. Our melanin and Latinidad are gifts of ancestors' dreaming, and nobody can take that away from us. I yearn for complication and stories untold. I yearn to hear his voice through a decolonial lens, separated from white colonial values and desires. And in this yearning, I must also accept the perhaps inevitable truth that even within my own community, there are no heroes. What has happened to Serafim's story highlights the importance of Black

† After Audre Lorde

communities writing our own stories, in our own words. If we don't do it, we run the risk of having our lives written for us, with parts of ourselves edited and erased to fit into colonial fantasies of terra nullius and peace.

[We will not be crunched into other people's fantasies and eaten alive.]

5 QUANTIFYING MELANIN

> Please try to remember that what they believe, as well as what they do and cause you to endure, does not testify to your inferiority, but to their inhumanity and fear.
>
> —JAMES BALDWIN

Despite his work ethic and his life-saving skill set, Serafim's Blackness had to constantly be lightened, excused, or erased to make his fanfare by Vancouverites socially acceptable. The majority of accounts at the turn of the century refer to him as either a "coloured," a "darkie," a "n-----," a "Negro," or "Old Black Joe," signalling that Serafim's Blackness was obvious to everyone, friend or foe.

Had Serafim been of a lighter complexion, he might have chosen to "pass" as something other than Black. Historically, many light-skinned individuals of African descent on Turtle Island have attempted to pass as non-Black for reasons of safety, status, or class ascension. Others have chosen to accept other people's racial classification of them as white or Indigenous for the same reasons. In *After Canaan,* Wayde Compton proposes the term *pheneticizing* to describe the action and power of assigning racial classification of an individual based on what the viewer perceives. This term recognizes the power imbalance between the viewer and the individual who is being classified. It also eliminates the suggestion of deception in the term *passing,* when an individual is assigned a racial category based on assumptions made from physical characteristics and without their being able to share their own identity in their own words. It is important to point out, however, that passing can be used as a tool of survival. As Compton explains, "Whether or not one has the right to transgress one's racial designation surely depends on the perniciousness of the regime that is policing the designations."[47] In Serafim's case, nothing suggests that he was pheneticized as anything other than a Black man, suggesting that he probably would not have been able to pass for anything other than Black, even if he'd desired to do so in an attempt to escape the societal racism of the time.

Since Serafim's Blackness was difficult to ignore by white citizens, the majority of writers throughout the twentieth and twenty-first centuries have highlighted his "unique" skin colour in what is perhaps an attempt to lighten him and set him apart from the racist minstrel depictions created by whites. Serafim's skin colour, however, was not unique, nor did he have any skin condition that would have made his skin distinct from that of other Black people. Serafim's skin tone is shared by millions across the Caribbean and Central and South America. These nations' histories and the multitude of skin tones within them have been largely shaped by the kidnapping and enslavement of Africans by Spaniards, beginning in the mid-1400s, to generate wealth for Spain, the Indigenous nations across the Caribbean islands and the South American continent, and the Spanish themselves. Most individuals throughout Central and South America and the Caribbean have mixed Indigenous, African, and Spanish ancestry, and as a result, we shine in every shade of melanin under the sun. Yet most authors at the turn of the century doted on the "uniqueness" of Serafim's skin colour:

> Joe had a nice round brown face and a beautiful brown body and arms and legs as he waded majestically in the waves of English Bay amongst all the little white lawyers and doctors and trained nurses and seamstresses who jumped up and down and splashed around him.[48]

> This mixed race parentage resulted in Joe's skin being chestnut brown, rather than the typically darker colouration of West Indians.[49]

Even as a Vancouver hero, Serafim has to be excused for his Blackness. Authors and journalists have written about him as if they were actively passing through an existential crisis to "excuse" him as a Black man. Articles praising his life and legacy are riddled with literary kneecaps such as "although," "in spite of," and "despite" to exceptionalize him, in an attempt to subvert the white supremacist status quo. Even at the 1927 unveiling of his memorial fountain, which Vancouverites paid out of pocket for, then Kiwanis president Charlie Bruce began his speech, "Under a dusky skin beat the heart of an unalloyed gold,"[50] suggesting that Serafim's skin colour somehow tarnished his pure heart and that one must look past his presumably evil and ugly Blackness to see his compassion for others.

Peter James Hudson points out in his essay "The Lost Tribe of a Lost Tribe" that Serafim's identity as a Black man was constantly erased in order for him to be accepted into white supremacist settler society. He cites the writing of Vancouver journalist Noel Robinson:

> It may be mentioned that Fortes was not a coal-black Negro—in fact he was not a Negro. He was a Barbadoan [sic] from Trinidad and was of very brown, tending to black complexion and may have had some Portuguese blood in his veins.[51]

Hudson highlights how Robinson attempts to erase Serafim's Blackness, first by interrupting his own racist generalization of Black individuals as having only "coal-black" skin tones, then by affirming that Serafim "was not a Negro." Robinson also reinforces colourism (prejudice that favours those with lighter skin tones over those with darker skin tones) by suggesting that having a darker skin tone would lower white settlers' perception of Serafim. It is important to highlight, once again, that there were other Black people living in Vancouver at the time who may very well have shared the same skin colour as Serafim. Although it is difficult to confirm his exact skin tone from black-and-white photographs, I assert again that it is in no way unique for Black individuals to be born with medium-brown complexions, regardless of their ancestry.

[My skin tone is one that shifts drastically from season to season, as my melanin rises in prominence to greet the sun or diminishes to rest in cooler seasons. Photos of my childhood and teenagehood, carefully laid out in thick photo albums on my mama's shelf, between framed arpilleras and Chilean pesos, tell the story of my childhood in all shades, in all seasons. In bright-pink snowsuits with three feet of snow, rich brown eyes and light-brown skin peeking out from hood and scarf; in floral playsuits, running on thick, cocoa-coloured legs through endless grass fields; or in blue-and-white shorts and T, an off-centre navy ball cap over dishevelled, textured hair, skin the shade of caramel, standing beside dinosaurs in Drumheller. I have always been me. And there has always been so much more to me than measuring and categorizing the amount of melanin in my body.]

In categorizing and classifying skin tone lies the danger of dehumanizing human beings, a practice with life-changing repercussions for Black people living in white supremacist societies worldwide. In the eyes of the white viewer who scrutinizes a single physical aspect of a Black person in a white supremacist society, the humanity of the Black individual ceases to exist; the individual becomes an animal or an object. No longer does the Black individual have a birth story, an upbringing, a favourite food or pastime. Their multiplicity of passions and heartbreaks is reduced to analysis of melanin and physical features, resulting in significant effects on their physical safety, socio-economic status, and lifespan. Eventually, this dehumanizing categorization process becomes rote, replicated across society without question. Imagine if the article by Noel Robinson were rewritten to reflect his own identity, in the same way he wrote about Serafim.

> It may be mentioned that Robinson was not an incandescent bright white—in fact he was not a white. He was a Brit from England and was of very neutral, tending to blanched complexion and may have had some Irish blood in his veins.

How does this excerpt now land, with the gaze reflected back onto the white writer? Robinson ceases to be a writer and instead, becomes an object. What would be the impact if we wrote about whites in the same manner that people of the global majority are written about?

This tendency toward dissecting, in a literary sense, the Black body has its origins in the dissection of the Black body in the *literal* sense. This can best be understood through the story of Saartjie Baartman, a Khoikhoi woman from the country now known as South Africa. Her tragic story begins with the death of her father at a young age and her entry into domestic service as a young, illiterate woman after a Dutch colonist murdered her partner. In service, she supposedly signed a contract with a British doctor to be displayed in shows that would eventually take her to England. She was exhibited in a cage so that onlookers could pay to see her buttocks, which were considered to be exceptionally large in size. She became known as the "Hottentot Venus." She was observed, touched, mocked, and made to wear a costume as she was paraded across London and Paris, until she died at age twenty-six of "eruptive inflammation" likely caused by pneumonia, syphilis, or alcoholism.[52]

What exactly were the contents of the contract she signed? How was this contract explained to this illiterate teenage girl? And even if it was adequately explained, how much did trauma and coercion play a role in her signing of the document? So much around this contract is lost to history, and given the context that *is* known, it seems apparent that no kind of consent was given. Particularly abhorrent is what happened to Saartjie's body after her death. When she passed in 1815, her body was dissected, with her brain and genitalia preserved to be put on display in

Paris's Museum of Man until 1974. It wasn't until 2002 that her remains were repatriated to her homeland and she was given a proper funeral.

Serafim didn't have to endure the misogyny and mutilation that Saartjie did. However, these two individuals did live in the same century, within active processes of colonization across the African continent, the Americas, and the Caribbean. The categorizations of Saartjie and Serafim were made without their own involvement, and both died without having told their own stories in their own words. What stories would Saartjie and Serafim want us to know? What would they tell us about themselves and who they were?

We will, unfortunately, never hear directly from these two individuals. The question I grapple with is how Serafim identified himself. Black? "Coloured"? British? Trinidadian? In 1911, he was listed in the census as speaking both Spanish and English, so he might even have identified as Afro Latino or "Negro" in Spanish. But we do know that many articles in Vancouver newspapers at the time of his death claimed that he had frequently proclaimed himself to be British.[53]

Although Trinidad was simply known as the British West Indies at the time, it surprises me to read these claims that Serafim identified only as British. Considering that his own father was a plantation worker in Trinidad and that Serafim was perhaps the first in his family line to be born free, he likely would have witnessed first-hand the impact of slavery under British rule for a significant portion of his life. Because of this, I have a hard time picturing him as having any kind of allegiance to the nation that likely enslaved his father. So, I wondered, where did the desire to proclaim a British identity come from?

First, given the propensity of white supremacist violence at the time, Serafim might have chosen to highlight his British identity in an attempt to fly under the radar of the ever-vigilant white settler gaze. It is also possible that he consciously espoused British pride in an attempt to fully assimilate into another British colony as a "real" British subject and to avoid facing scrutiny, as many newcomers to Canada still do. Another consideration is that many people of Caribbean descent embrace the Jamaican motto, "Out of many, one people," which conveys that the history and the mixed heritage of the island make it what it is today. If Serafim held this adage as true, it might have made sense for him to drop the "West Indies" portion and just say he was British, to avoid a complex explanation of race, place, and ancestry.

Dissatisfied with the claims about Serafim's British pride, I searched deeper in the British Columbia newspaper archives between 1900 and his death in 1922 to see if I could find direct quotes of him identifying as British. I noticed that for the most part, whenever he was quoted directly, Serafim asserted that he was from either Trinidad or the British *West Indies*. It is important to note here that he does not drop the West Indies portion; this raises my suspicions as to whether this portion was dropped by the people who wrote about him.

Serafim was even known to "shock" American tourists on the beach by informing them that he was from the British West Indies and not from the United States, as many tourists assumed him to be. When he passed away in 1922, dedications in his honour poured into all major newspaper outlets. All commended the "British-coloured" lifeguard, thus beginning many decades of journalists repeating this convenient omission when writing about his life.

I could find only three instances where Serafim was directly quoted as proclaiming his British identity. The first was when he arrived in Vancouver in 1885 and a fellow sailor attempted to deceive him; he was reported to have said he was a British sailor and couldn't be fooled.[54] Here, he appeared to use his identity to assert his intelligence and status. The second instance was in 1910, during a bartending shift at the Bodega Hotel, when he encountered a "Yankee captain" who demanded immediate service. According to the article, the man yelled, "When are you going to attend to me you d----d [n-----]?"[55†] Serafim ignored the man and continued

† Note that the word *damned* is censored for profanity in this account, but n----- is not.

serving other patrons. The man's anger escalated, and he became more and more aggressive. Finally, Serafim calmly walked over, grabbed him by the collar, and said, "Now I'll attend to you sir. I'll have you know that I'm a British subject, and that's a better man than you are." He then threw the man out the door, threatening that there would be trouble if he were to return. In this instance, Serafim used his British identity to assert dominance in the hotel and to secure a relative degree of safety.

The third instance was during an event that same year when the city honoured him with an "Illuminated Address," a certificate of appreciation; he ended his speech with a boisterous "God save the King!"[56] Perhaps in this instance, Serafim used the public speaking opportunity to further assert his loyalty to colonial rule and build up his reputation as a model Negro citizen, thus maintaining his relative level of safety within a white supremacist society, just three years after the anti-Asian riots in Vancouver's downtown core. Conversely, this proclamation could also reveal that he truly saw himself as equal to other white settlers, without any anticolonial analysis or sentiment at play.

To me, the biggest tragedy of Serafim Fortes's life is that he will never be able to tell us in his own words who he was. His legacy will forever be shaped by what the white imagination desired him to be. I strongly believe that Serafim did indeed understand the importance of writing his own story, as in an interview with Noel Robinson he stopped answering questions and said he was keeping more details for his "little book," which he then revealed in the pocket of his waistcoat. Perhaps he didn't trust the reporter with the most intimate details of his life, or perhaps he didn't want his words to be twisted. Whatever the case may be, the little book was never located after his death, and so, as it is with many other Black histories, what we know of his life is shaped by the thoughts, observations, and opinions of the people who had the power to hold pen and publish: white settlers.

The recounting of Serafim's life (or the imagining of who he was) is further evidence that what is written and archived by those in the dominant group is what becomes accepted as history by the dominant group. No matter what biases the archivist or writer holds, their perspective is the one that becomes Truth, further entrenching settler colonial narratives for the nation state they belong to, as well as the justification for violence and displacement of those outside of the dominant group.

A 1913 Vancouver postcard found on November 24, 2022, alongside other photos of Joe Fortes smiling at the beach. The handwriting on the back reads, "Vancouver, BC. The [n-----] is a lifesaver at English Bay, — has rescued many people from drowning. Love R."†

† This image was originally retrieved from the Vancouver Heritage Foundation's Places That Matter website. During my research, I was shocked to see that it was prominently displayed as one of three images of his person. I posted the screenshot of this image on my Instagram account, and shortly afterward it was brought to the attention of the Vancouver Heritage Foundation. In a publicly posted comment, their team responded to my post: "This postcard from 1913 contains historical racist language and should not have been shared without a warning and contextual information that addressed the racist language. We apologize for any harm caused by including the postcard on our site without warning and context and we will make sure to carefully review and contextualize all historical content we include in our website in the future." The image has since been removed from the website.

6 JOE FORTES, MODEL NEGRO CITIZEN

Suppose that Serafim Fortes was a white man.

Would he have been seen as exceptional?

Suppose that Serafim, as a Black man, chose to set up camp farther east on the inlet and interacted only with Indigenous and racialized communities.

Would he have been seen as exceptional?

Suppose it was only Indigenous and racialized communities that Serafim had taught how to swim and that it just so happened it was only their lives that he saved.

Would he have been seen as exceptional?

Suppose that Serafim is considered exceptional only because of whose lives he saved.

Does it then mean that some lives are valued more than others?

Are the lives he saved what makes him exceptional?

The permanent contradiction in the acceptance of Serafim Fortes as a Black man and a beloved hero cannot be understood without delving into the societal context of the turn of the twentieth century.

Serafim made a name for himself just one year after his arrival in Vancouver for his help in evacuating citizens during the Great Fire of 1886. Years later, he rose to prominence again for saving the life of the American vice-consul at Íy̓el̓shn.[57] As one article in the Windsor *Evening Record* explains,

> Col. Cook, American consul at Dawson, has asked that an effort be made to secure the Humane Society medal for the coloured man, Joe Fortes, bartender at the Alhambra Hotel, Vancouver, who saved from drowning Vice-Consul Burke of Dawson, at English Bay, Vancouver, by diving for him when he disappeared for the last time. Fortes had saved six human lives in as many years at Vancouver's bathing resort, English Bay, and he deserves the medal far more than many of those who have for it.[58]

Although Serafim had been working as a lifeguard for years at this point, his saving of the vice-consul's life seems to have proliferated his popularity in Vancouver and finally validated his role as a lifeguard. Consul Cook goes so far as to say that others who have received the award in the past, namely whites, are not as deserving as Serafim—a statement that surely would have turned heads, given the open subjugation of Black communities at this time.

The article ends abruptly by providing a small window into Serafim's awareness of anti-Black racism at the systemic level in Canadian society, concluding that "'Joe' thinks the Humane Society has drawn the colour line on him," which directly contradicts the reputation that "Joe" was easy to please and always ready to serve, as well as the assumption that Serafim wasn't acutely aware of the anti-Black racism that he navigated in Vancouver.

The only other window into Serafim's true feelings about living in settler society that I came across was published in the October 14, 1903, edition of the *Vancouver Daily Province* about the first Thanksgiving holiday in Canada. Prominent Vancouver citizens were asked what they were thankful for, and between other responses about being thankful to be alive or, conversely, not dead, Serafim responds, "That the kiddies have stopped coming to the beach."[59†] Once again, this stands in stark contrast to the reputation or, dare I say, *fantasy*, of Serafim being always ready to serve without complaint. Although he did genuinely seem to enjoy teaching

† Note that Serafim is quoted in plain English here, without any grammatical errors or a "Southern" accent.

children how to swim, he too grew tired and needed time to himself, not being in service of others.

Many Vancouver citizens were indeed aware of Serafim's invaluable service to the city. In 1900, a petition began circulating, appealing to the municipal government to provide Serafim with a salary in exchange for his lifeguard duties.[60] Just a few years after the petition to pay Serafim was presented to city council, downtown Vancouver streets were lined with a mob of armed white men holding large banners that read "Stand for a White Canada," their loud chants and singing of "The Maple Leaf Forever" reverberating against storefront windows. Among these men were prominent politicians, policemen, and wealthy businessmen.

The mob headed to Japantown and Chinatown to smash the windows of Japanese- and Chinese-owned businesses and homes and threaten the lives of individuals of East Asian descent. The year was 1907. Serafim's home remained safe.

One year later, the Vancouver Opera House hosted *The Clansman*, a play based on Thomas Dixon Jr.'s "Historical Romance of the Ku Klux

Smashed storefronts in the aftermath of the Anti-Asian Riots of 1907. | Japanese Canadian Research Collection, UBC Library JCPC-36-024

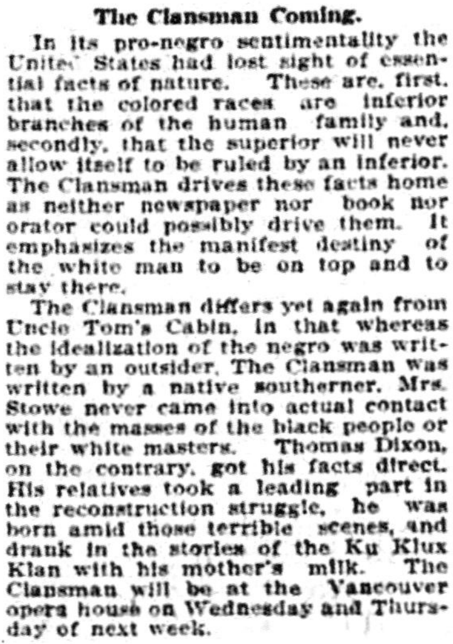

The Clansman Coming.

In its pro-negro sentimentality the United States had lost sight of essential facts of nature. These are, first, that the colored races are inferior branches of the human family and, secondly, that the superior will never allow itself to be ruled by an inferior. The Clansman drives these facts home as neither newspaper nor book nor orator could possibly drive them. It emphasizes the manifest destiny of the white man to be on top and to stay there.

The Clansman differs yet again from Uncle Tom's Cabin, in that whereas the idealization of the negro was written by an outsider, The Clansman was written by a native southerner. Mrs. Stowe never came into actual contact with the masses of the black people or their white masters. Thomas Dixon, on the contrary, got his facts direct. His relatives took a leading part in the reconstruction struggle, he was born amid those terrible scenes, and drank in the stories of the Ku Klux Klan with his mother's milk. The Clansman will be at the Vancouver opera house on Wednesday and Thursday of next week.

Excerpt of a review of *The Clansman* at the Vancouver Opera House. | *Vancouver Daily Province*, 1908

Klan (KKK)," on its fourth record-setting tour, which captivated over four million people across Canada and the United States. The show sold out, Serafim continued to save whites at Íy̓el̓shn, and he continued to receive high praise for his work ethic and skill set.

The year was 1908. Serafim was safe.

Serafim's home was safe.

Serafim was safe.

Under six elm trees, Serafim was safe.

But why?

[To my best friend in grade three, my only Black friend in elementary school: I'm sorry there were no elm trees to keep your house safe. I didn't know what it meant when they threw a brick through your living room window just months after you moved in. I thought that maybe it was a prank. I never understood why no other house on the block got pranked. Your mother never said anything when I asked why. Maybe now, I will gift you an elm tree.]

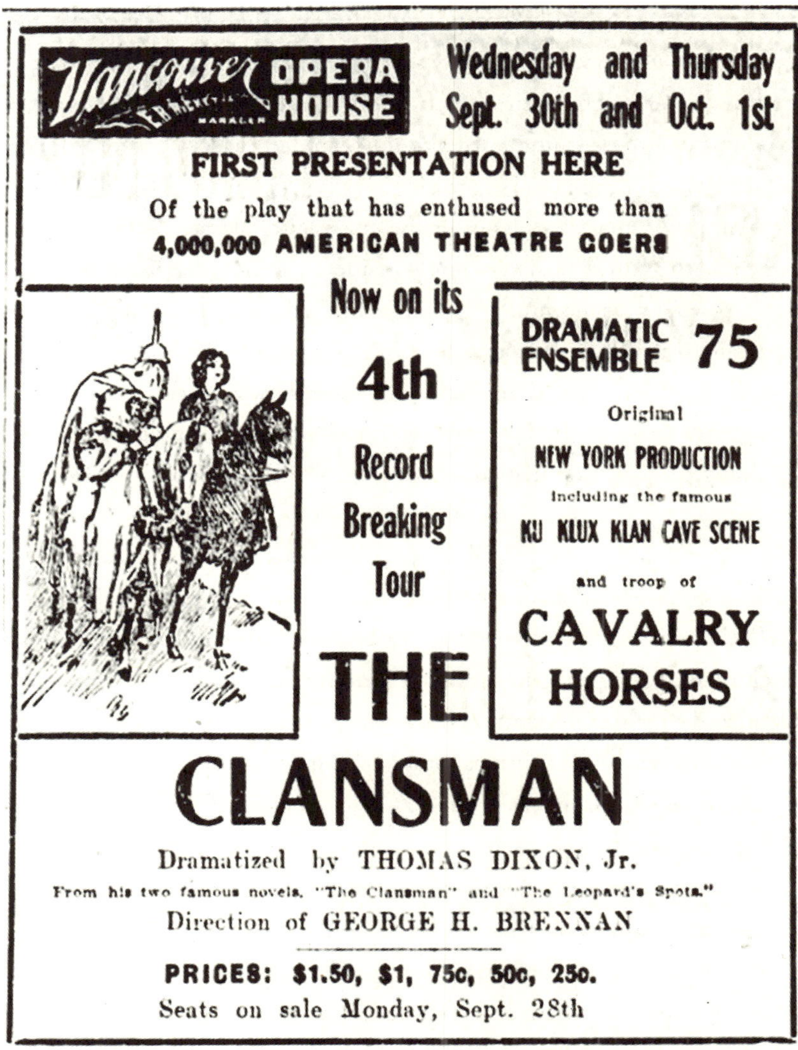

A newspaper advertisement for *The Clansman*.† | *Vancouver Daily World*, September 30, 1908

† The 1915 film *The Birth of a Nation* was based on this play. Samuel Howard and Charles Scurry penned a petition on behalf of the Black community to ban the film in Vancouver, but the show still went on. *The Birth of a Nation* is said to have incited a rise in lynchings across the US and to have helped spark the resurgence of the KKK in Canada.

Critic Peter James Hudson proposes that Serafim "was assumable into Vancouver's white culture in a way that the Asian population—because of the fears generated by their numerical preponderance and their potential economic clout—was not. Fortes could become a mascot because Asians had remained a menace," suggesting that what shielded Serafim from the white supremacist violence of the era was the voracity of anti-Asian hatred at the time.[61] Asians were considered a menace simply because their growing presence in the Lower Mainland, both physically and economically, threatened the social positioning of whites. I would also suggest that Serafim's (mis)use of his special constable's badge to discriminate and assault members of the Chinese community, and the public's praise for his doing so, is what shielded him from the white supremacist violence of the era.

So, then, was every strong Black sporting hero safe, even if outnumbered? Was every gentle, acquiescent working-class Black person safe?

Perhaps the greatest challenge to Serafim's exceptionalism as both Black man and sporting hero was in March 1909, when Jack Johnson, a Texan and the first Black world heavyweight boxing champion, arrived in Vancouver dressed to the nines for an exhibition match at the Vancouver Athletic Club. Johnson was greeted by a giant crowd of fans and reporters all eager to catch a glimpse of him. But, unfortunately for Johnson, his achievements and his smooth demeanour did not help him secure a place to rest his head in Vancouver.

Just a few months earlier, Johnson had made history when Tommy Burns, a white Canadian, accepted his challenge to fight him in Sydney, Australia. For the first time in history, a Black man would share the boxing ring with a white man. Up until this point, boxing matches had been racially segregated in an attempt to maintain power within white communities. These segregated boxing matches asserted whites as dominant in the social hierarchy and ensured that peak physical strength and athleticism could never be represented in anybody who wasn't white.

Thousands of fans in Sydney came out to see the match, with police nearby, fearful of what might unfold. More fans across the nation tuned in to watch. Tensions were high. After Burns made racist remarks, Johnson responded swiftly and heavily, leaving the white boxer almost motionless on the ground. Television transmissions ended abruptly, and police were called to control the situation in the ring and in the audience. Jack Johnson became the world heavyweight champion.

In the months after the fight, the KKK began a search for the "Great White Hope" who would reclaim the heavyweight boxing champion title, but Johnson paid them no mind. He dressed in expensive clothing, fearlessly flirted with white women, and was seemingly unaffected by white supremacist threats and policies at the time. In other words, he lived with dignity.

So when Jack Johnson and his wife attempted to check in at Vancouver's new St. Francis Hotel—boasting modern suites and the best

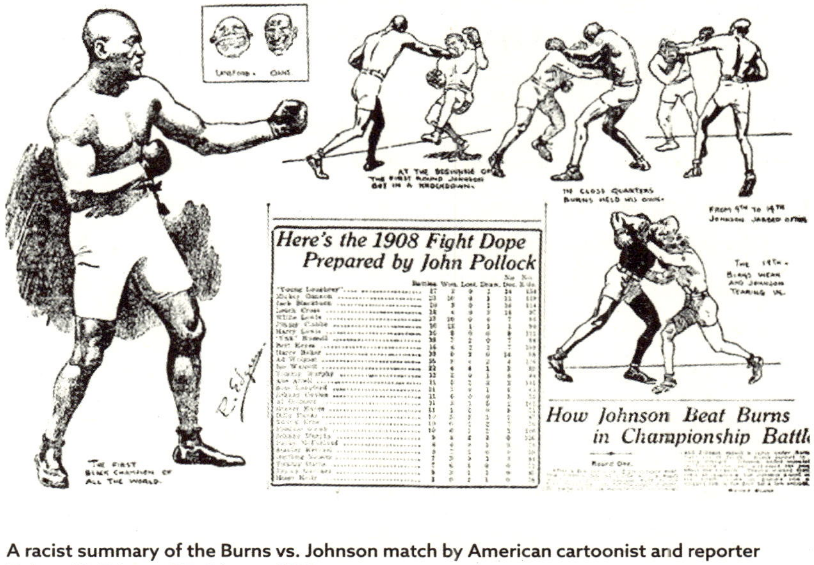

A racist summary of the Burns vs. Johnson match by American cartoonist and reporter Robert W. Edgren. | R. Edgren, 1908

location in the city—one could have assumed that he would be greeted with a warm welcome equal to the fanfare he'd received earlier in the day. But this was not the case. To Johnson's surprise, he and his wife were barred from checking in.

Undeterred, Johnson and his wife went to the newly built Irving Hotel, only to be met with the same treatment. Next, the world heavyweight champion attempted to check in at the Rainier on Carrall Street, only a few minutes away, and once again, he was turned away at the door. There were rooms available, but none were available to him. Johnson continued his search for lodging at the Metropole and the Astor, to no avail.

The press, the doting fans, and all the fanfare of the day seemed to have disappeared by nightfall. The love that so many Vancouverites claimed to have for Serafim, another Black sports celebrity of sorts, did not translate into hospitality for Johnson.

Finally, after who knows how many wasted hours and incidents of anti-Black racism along the way, Johnson was able to contact George Paris, another Black man who was a trainer at the Vancouver Athletic Club. Paris welcomed Johnson and his wife into his home. The next day, the *Vancouver Daily Province* printed a sensational headline about Johnson, boasting a "Great Reception for the Big Black."

> Anyone who thinks this same Jack Johnson is an ignorant and unsophisticated Negro should have seen the Chesterfieldian grace with which he bade farewell to those ladies in silks and satins on the *Makura* yesterday.[62]

Here is yet another example of writers of the time contradicting themselves by praising Blackness in the same breath as propagating the racist stereotypes they themselves created.

If not for Johnson's visit to the city, one could only have speculated on whether or not Serafim was truly an exceptional Negro in the eyes of white society. But with two Black men, both athletic, both champions within their respective sports, occupying the same space at the same time, it is easy to point out contradictions and find the differences in their treatment. So, what exactly made Johnson and Serafim so different?

Serafim was stout, modest, and "eager to please." Johnson, on the other hand, was muscular, tall, confident, and, most importantly, had unmatched prowess in the boxing ring that whites saw as the capacity to physically dominate and potentially kill white men. In other words, Johnson was a threat to white supremacy. As American historian Jeffrey Sammons points out, "Johnson represented the 'bad [n-----]' that whites were so willing to parade as an example of why Blacks must be kept in 'their place.'"[63]

So what would have happened if Fortes and Johnson had stood together? Would they all of a sudden have been perceived as a threat to society? Would all of Serafim's actions of bravery and self-sacrifice have stood for nothing in the eyes of Vancouver residents because he was no longer the only Black person at English Bay? Or would he have ceased to be perceived as subservient simply by association with Johnson?

I constantly stand in awe at the mental gymnastics needed to make the fanfare for Serafim socially acceptable, but then I reflect upon my own experiences growing up as an Afro Latina in Alberta and think that maybe things haven't changed very much at all. Growing up as a teenager, I was one of two Black people in the Edmonton punk scene. The punk scene for me felt like the only place where I fit in.

amiskwaciy (Edmonton), Treaty 6, is the traditional territory of the Nêhiyaw, Niitsitapi, Métis, Stoney Nakoda, and Dene peoples. In the 1870s, a series of numbered treaties with British Crown representatives were signed under duress by Indigenous nations across the Prairies. These displaced thousands of Indigenous communities onto reserves and allowed for the settlement of the Prairies primarily by people of Eastern European descent. The Prairies were advertised as the "land of milk and honey" and "the Last Best West."

The process of colonization across the Prairies persisted in the later decades through various laws restricting the immigration of people of African descent and instead offering opportunities for Europeans to settle on the newly stolen lands. Throughout the 1970s and '80s, a major oil boom attracted a large population of migrants from across the world to work in the tar sands and service industries. Conservative governments reigned, decade after decade, mirroring a socially conservative environment.

I grew up in that socially conservative environment, just like Serafim did. I was almost always the only Black person in my class and always the only Afro Latina person in my school. The Catholic schools I attended on the south end primarily attracted families from wealthy backgrounds, while my single mother was barely able to make ends meet.

So when I discovered punk music in grade nine, it changed my life. Being a misfit, being poor, and thinking for yourself were all things welcomed in the culture. "Angry, Young and Poor" by Anti-Flag became my anthem, and it shielded me from the laughter and mockery of my classmates. Within a couple months, I was going to punk shows every weekend, and I met a whole new group of friends who accepted me for who I was. Most of them, anyway.

Most of the kids I was hanging out with were white. We would dance to ska, shove each other with love in the mosh pit, and drink beers in minus-thirty-five-degree weather outside shows. We wore leather jackets, and our pants were riddled with holes and the patches of our favourite punk bands: the Devotchkas, the Homewreckers, Crass, GBH, and DIRT. Some other "friends" sported patches for Skrewdriver, a white supremacist band from England, and the occasional swastika on their pants leg.

At first I ignored the swastikas and the Skrewdriver patches. Pushed it out of my mind. It didn't really matter. By then I was sixteen, and heck, I knew these were good people. We went to shows together, covered each other for tickets and bus fare. I often found myself sipping beer and singing old punk songs right across from skinheads who I later found out were active members of the Aryan Guard, a white supremacist group actively recruiting across the Prairies. I remember once gathering the courage to ask one white punk "friend," in the bathroom of our favourite late-night pizza joint, why she wore her Skrewdriver patch but also hung out with me.

She looked at me, smiled, and said, "It's different, Ruby. You're cool." I laughed it off, went back to our booth, and we finished our pizza and beer.

I never faced physical violence. And as far as we know, no incidents of physical violence toward Serafim in Vancouver were ever documented either. But why?

Maybe it was because just like Serafim, I was the only Black person in that place at that time and thus, was seen as not a threat, easy to surveil and control. For both Serafim and myself, I would argue that our docility in our day-to-day existence and our ability to bond over meaningful experiences with the dominant group also allowed us to make it through unscathed. Serafim was known to be modest and "always willing," and because of this, his presence was "approved in every household in Vancouver."[64]

In addition, I would argue that Serafim was shielded by white supremacist violence because of the raw magnitude he had on people's lives by rescuing them from death. *Who* he rescued also mattered. Rescuing prominent white politicians and affluent whites undoubtedly had won the hearts of those who were calling the shots in Vancouver at the time. Rescuing an American vice-consul caused him to gain even more prominence. Serafim might have been less shielded from white supremacist violence had he saved only Black, Indigenous, or Chinese people.

In a similar vein, whites *depended* on Serafim's role in the water for their own survival and the survival of their children; this in turn may have preserved his personhood. This parasitic dynamic is seen across Turtle Island and the Caribbean, wherever whites enslaved Black communities or relied on Black communities to generate wealth. As Trinidadian-born writer C.L.R. James describes,

> while the propertied whites here allow the Negroes a certain freedom, they do not need them for labor and are therefore indifferent to Negro persecution by the poor whites. In the Black Belt, however, the plantation

> owners protect their Negro serfs from the hostility of the poor whites. They are not going to have their labor force interfered with by a rival labor force. When there is any lynching to be done, they themselves will do it, in a systematic and organized manner ... Between 1900 and 1930, whenever the price of cotton is above the usual trend, the number of lynchings is below the average. Whenever the price of cotton is depressed, the number of lynchings increases.[65]

All in all, it is difficult to truly pinpoint what exactly affords safety to individuals in white supremacist contexts, as it would be impossible to know each white settler's mindset and motivations. I would argue that it is a case-by-case basis, with each involved township, city, time period, person, and personality converging and yielding different results every time.

For Serafim and me, maybe it was all of the above. Or maybe it was just luck.

We'll never really know.

7 ON LOVE AND BEING LOVED

> Awakening to love can happen only as we let go of our obsession with power and domination.
> —bell hooks

Canadian society has historically been and continues to be a swinging pendulum between feigned tolerance and outward aggression toward Indigenous peoples and racialized communities. While Canada claims to embrace being a "mosaic" that highly values multiculturalism and religious pluralism, its politicians and citizens have often actioned the opposite. Canada's history of intolerance begins even before Confederation in 1867, but the creation of the 1876 Indian Act that aimed to "civilize," Christianize, and assimilate Indigenous peoples, primarily through the systematic kidnapping and brutalizing of children in residential schools, land theft and segregation policies enacted through reserves, and the elimination of status through disenfranchisement, ensured that Canada's intolerance toward Indigenous nations would be enshrined within its constitution.

Throughout the late 1800s, Canada amplified migration restrictions and expulsions of specific racial groups. The head tax under the Chinese Immigration Act of 1885 targeted Chinese communities and required Chinese migrants to pay fees upon entry to Canada—from fifty dollars to five hundred dollars between 1885 and 1903. The "continuous voyage regulation" in 1908 barred all Asian migrants from entering Canada unless their ship had made a continuous journey from the place of their citizenship origin. Since no ships from South Asia at the time could make it to Canada in one continuous journey, South Asian citizens were effectively shut out. In addition, South Asians migrants were required to pay a head tax of two hundred dollars—eight times more than white migrants.[66]

In 1913, Vancouverites came out en masse to celebrate the life of Mohawk poet Tekahionwake (E. Pauline Johnson). Tekahionwake grew up away from her community, and her work often romanticized Indigenous people by using "noble savage" tropes. She gained popularity by beginning her performances dressed in traditional regalia, then switching to Victorian-style dress. Her funeral was the largest of the century, and a monument was erected in X̱wáýx̱way (Stanley Park) in her name. Later that year, the City of Vancouver forcibly displaced Squamish residents from Seṅáḵw, where present-day Vanier Park is located, but the city loved Tekahionwake.

In 2021, the Royal Canadian Mounted Police (RCMP) wore orange shirts to observe the National Day for Truth and Reconciliation, which mourns the missing and murdered Indigenous children sent to residential schools by the Canadian government, the Catholic Church, and RCMP officers, and to acknowledge the call to action to ensure that this genocide will never happen again. Today, travellers arriving at the Vancouver International Airport see captivating billboards advertising the rich cultural history of Indigenous nations in so-called British Columbia. Nowhere on these billboards is it evident that, in November 2020, the RCMP invaded the unceded territories of the Wet'suwet'en Nation. Armed with guns, axes, attack dogs, and sniper rifles, the police arrested peaceful land defenders who were asserting their rights as protected under the UN Declaration on the Rights of Indigenous Peoples and the 1997 *Delgamuukw v. British Columbia* ruling. All of this to push a natural gas pipeline through the territory for the economic benefit of the settler nation of Canada. Travellers arriving in Vancouver for the very first time might get the impression that the province holds a deep reverence for all Indigenous nations and even loves them, just like they "loved" Serafim.

In 2020, a Black father by the name of George Floyd was killed by police officer Derek Chauvin in Minneapolis, Minnesota. Hundreds of thousands of people across Canada rose up to protest, decrying police brutality, demanding the defunding of the police, and calling for systemic change regarding anti-Black racism. Individuals, businesses, and organizations posted black squares on social media profiles. Racist public figures were called out, including white country singer Morgan Wallen, who was caught on tape using the N-word while on a seventy-two-hour bender. Hundreds of organizations across the continent manufactured elaborate media campaigns, proposing their front-facing commitment to social change. The message across Turtle Island rang out loud and clear: never again.

As I write this in 2023, I see that not much has changed. Black squares on social media quickly disappeared a few months after George Floyd's murder, and police departments across Turtle Island have by and large *increased* their funding, claiming the need for "public safety."[67] Body cameras now record police murders, capture the faces of passersby into facial recognition databases, and seem to be plagued by glitches, power outages, and pesky uniforms covering lenses in the most critical moments. The NHL pledges "Hockey for All," refusing accountability for racist incidents in the league, while Morgan Wallen saw a 1,220 percent increase in digital album sales and a 327 percent increase in song sales in the days after his tape was released. He later went on to win the 2023 Billboard Music Award for best country album of the year.[68]

George Floyd's daughter still goes to bed every night without her father. An entire nation's vow to never let something so violent come to pass again didn't last longer than a couple months.

So why does North American society claim to love the very communities that it seeks to control and eliminate? Because this isn't love at all. As feminist writer bell hooks explains, "Abuse and neglect negate love ... No one can rightfully claim to be loving when behaving abusively."[69]

In Canada, the settler colonial state has been behaving abusively since before it even officially became a nation, and it continues to behave as such. The entire premise of this country relies on the racist Doctrine of Discovery issued by the Vatican in 1493, which asserts that anyone who is not Christian is to be subdued, vanquished, and destroyed and that all "moveable and inmovable goods" should be captured.[70]

Our entire country relies on theft and subjugation as its premise. So, as a society, we have never known what it is to love.

Now consider this: many whites at the turn of the nineteenth century likely believed that Serafim Fortes truly was their friend. I counter this with a question: was there truly love present for Serafim?

A friend, I would argue, is someone with whom we build a relationship based in mutual trust, care, respect, and love. Acquaintances, by contrast, are relationships based on circumstance that do not deepen to the extent a friendship does.

A friend enters your home and spends time there at ease. An acquaintance visits in a public space and, soon after, in unspoken ritual, leaves. I believe that a true marker of the "love" for Serafim Fortes can be found in whose homes he entered. Which friends' homes was he welcomed into?

In my research I was only able to locate evidence of two homes that Serafim entered: the Scurry family home and the Carrol, Thompson, and Mckenzie home. The Scurry family, an African Estadounidenses* family from the United States, had arrived in Vancouver in 1886, around the same time as Serafim. The patriarch, Hiram Scurry, was formerly enslaved and first settled in Winnipeg with his wife, Martha (originally from Ontario), and their kids before trying his luck in Vancouver.[71] The couple first ran a popular barbershop and were responsible for forming the first barbers' union in Vancouver. When Hiram passed away in 1895, Martha opened up a rooming house on Cambie Street. Serafim stayed here during the winter season until he moved to Íy̓el̓shn to provide lifeguard services for Vancouver residents on a full-time basis.

There is no documentation about how or when Serafim came to meet the Scurry family, one of only two Black families living in Vancouver at the time. In one of my imaginings, the township fades away into cobblestone as Martha and Hiram lock eyes with Serafim amid a sea of mostly white settler faces, spellbound, all three recognizing each other's untold stories. The spell is cast over and over again in decades to come, under overpasses, in railway stations, in the hot, cramped kitchens of five-star restaurants—wherever we may find each other, Black kin, on stolen homelands far from a long-ago home. A hundred years later, I find myself silently locking eyes with other kin of African descent on Vancouver streets. Sometimes exchanging fleeting smiles, sometimes knowing looks in exasperating situations, or sometimes simply a nod or a hello, reminding us of a shared journey long ago from an ocean away.

[Enter Ruby, a six-year-old girl in pigtail braids, blue jeans, a denim shirt, and pink rubber boots, and her dad in jeans, sneakers, and a nylon windbreaker. Ruby clutches her dad's hand and tries to keep up as they walk through the corridor of a south end mall in amiskwaciy. They pass a tall Black man, and he and Ruby's dad lock eyes, nodding at each other. Ruby's dad lets out a small smile.

"Dad, who was that guy you nodded to?"

"Me nuh know."

"So you didn't know him?"

(smiling faintly) "Me know him long ago."]

In one fold in time, Serafim connected with Martha in the hallways of her rooming house, between guest arrivals and departures, as they shared experiences of discrimination in confidence, each knowing that the other would understand. This ritual repeated week after week, eventually transforming into friendship.

What we know for sure is that his friendship with the Scurry family withstood the test of time; even after Serafim was granted a cabin, the Scurry family visited him in his home at Íỷeḯshn. In a personal account of her friendship with Serafim, Martha's granddaughter, Goldvine, recalled that she was always welcomed in and treated to sweets and tea. As she relates, there were "two ladies that liked to call on [Joe] while out for their evening stroll," and Serafim told Goldvine and her grandmother to freeze and stay quiet so as to not alert the two ladies that he was at home.[72] Once the two women had left, Serafim revealed that he didn't like to be interrupted when visiting with "his people." From Serafim's description of Goldvine and the Howard family as "his people," it is safe to assume that the two ladies who liked to visit him at his cabin were not Black. This offers a window into Serafim's personal life: despite his being described as "eager to please," he considered time with "his people" to be precious and worth protecting.

Perhaps Serafim's cabin at Íỷeḯshn transformed into a fortress against white supremacy when the Scurry family visited. His fortress, which he guarded with love, was a fold in space and time among elm trees and the West End forest. Given the overt white supremacist violence at the time, being at home was perhaps the only space where he didn't have to fear for his life if he said or did the wrong thing.

Much like Serafim, the times when I can connect with other folks of African descent in Vancouver are few and far in between, even a century later. Those rare times become fortresses where I can let my guard down and speak from the heart without worrying how my thoughts and actions may be perceived by the white viewer. They are spaces where I can laugh as hard as I want without judgment and, for a brief moment, not have to defend my lived experiences against a litany of questions. These fortresses I protect with every ounce of my being in order to preserve my softness.

The only other documented time when Serafim was invited to a home was on September 8, 1900. This visit was reported in the *Vancouver Daily Province*. Serafim visited the "open house" of the Carrol, Thompson, and

Mckenzie household. Along with a handful of other guests, he spent the evening playing cards, enjoying music, and sharing "delicacies," and he ended the night by sharing that "he would always remember this pleasant evening and hoped that all present would endeavour to do what they could to purchase this beautiful beach."[73] The open house setting suggests that, although the gathering did indeed take place within a home, it was considered a public event rather than a private dinner among family and friends. Additionally, Serafim's presence at the event was perhaps more of a transactional one, where Serafim was able to pitch the purchase of stolen land in order to secure "protection" for his beloved beach and where, perhaps, the families were able to show off their affiliation with a Black man as a way to elevate their social status.

The showing off of proximity to Blackness as status symbol was nothing new to white settlers in Canada. As Robyn Maynard writes in *Policing Black Lives*, "It is enormously significant that Black subjection played such an important role in white social status ... That 'fashion' included the day-to-day violence inherent in enslaving a human being demonstrates the economically *and* culturally significant role that Black confinement and dehumanization played for white settlers."[74]

Photographs of Serafim from this time period can be seen through the lens of white settlers wanting to show off their proximity to him, or, as Peter James Hudson proposes, treating him almost as a mascot. It is critical to note that in photos of Serafim taken in public spaces outside of the water, he is never sitting or standing shoulder to shoulder with any whites. This suggests that, although he was known and respected as a public Vancouver figure, he was in no way welcome to breach the white supremacist order through physical contact outside of a meticulously calculated and surveilled interaction in his role as a lifeguard.

To find more evidence of informal segregation on English Bay Beach between the 1900s and '20s, I examined photos of the beach in the City of Vancouver Archives. Due to the low quality of photography from the period and their only being available in black and white, I found it difficult

Serafim is seated in close proximity with a group of white beachgoers at Íỷeḷshn, but his position on the rowboat speaks volumes. He sits at the very end, suggesting he was the last to sit, and significantly farther away from the rest of the group, denoting a lack of trust and highlighting the racial divide around physical contact. | City of Vancouver Archives, AM1376-: CVA 1376-227

to be able to pheneticize individuals in the long shots of crowds. In close-ups, I could only find individuals who appear to be white.

I once again turned to newspaper archives to see if I could uncover any information about non-white communities after the popularization of Íỷeḷshn. One headline caught my attention: it had to do with two Chinese men at the English Bay bathhouse in June 1906, and Serafim Fortes was at the centre of it. According to Serafim, he had "caught" a Chinese man in the locker room "after hours," which roused his suspicion. Because of how much time has lapsed since the turn of the century, it is hard to know what the official hours of the bathhouse were, if any. Nevertheless, the manner in which the interaction unfolds suggests that the presence of Chinese individuals was not a regular occurrence at English Bay.

"I told them three times to move, but they said they had money and would do as they pleased. They thought they could bluff me, but let me tell you they can't bluff this chicken! I am a constable and I am going to see that things are all right around here!"

Serafim claimed to have caught the men stealing,[75] and he physically assaulted them. In court, when pressed about his use of physical force, he first denied having touched the men. Upon further questioning, he admitted to using a "little shove" to assert his authority and defended his actions, proclaiming, "They have a right to behave themselves, but they have no right to run the town. They can't run this constable, anyway."

This incident underscores Serafim's role in maintaining and enforcing settler colonial rule—despite belonging to a racial group that was systemically marginalized—and shows him proudly doing so. His discriminatory actions were approved of by settlers, as evidenced by the article's opening: "It is evident that Joe Fortes, the good-natured coloured cop who guards English Bay Beach, is not to be trifled with, especially by a Chinaman." I wonder, how could Serafim have maintained the contradiction of enforcing segregation policies? If he was indeed the only Black man seen in the space, and having experienced racist assaults first-hand, could he not see that he was perpetrating the very acts that could easily be done to him?

Serafim's role in maintaining and enforcing settler colonial rule is even documented outside of English Bay; he racially profiled and assaulted a Chinese man by the name of Sing, who Serafim claimed was attempting to break into a house on Burnaby Street while carrying a butcher cart. Serafim was praised by the court for "preventing the commission of a crime," but when pressed about whether or not he had actually seen Sing break in, Serafim exclaimed, "Break in? Do you think I would let him break in? Why I never let him get near enough. I was there to keep him from breakin' in." Sing's lawyer countered that his client was just trying to reach the front door of the residence to ask for a job when he was assaulted by Serafim. In the end, the case was dismissed.[76]

With the anti-Asian exclusion policy circulating that very year, in 1904, and the crowds proclaiming their desire for a "white Canada," did Serafim not look on these Chinese men as individuals being targeted by the same white supremacist forces that also targeted Black people? How and why did he consider himself to be the exception?

It is important to highlight that, despite Serafim's presence as a Black man on the beach or, as one article puts it, "a large-sized chocolate drop with red stripes around it, bobbing up and down in the water," there is little evidence to support that other Black people were ever present or welcome at English Bay.[77] It is unclear whether or not English Bay was an officially segregated space, but there is plenty of evidence in the archives to support the notion that only certain Vancouver neighbourhoods tolerated the presence of non-white people. Vancouver's community of Park Lane, better known as Hogan's Alley, for example, came into prominence in 1930 and was a predominantly non-white community, with most of its residents being Jewish, Chinese, or Black. For Black communities, the area became an increasingly attractive place to live, first for its proximity to the train line, where many Black men were employed as porters, and second because it was one of the few places where Black people felt at home in Vancouver. Fountain Chapel Church, which was the heart of the Black community up until Hogan's Alley was demolished by the City of Vancouver in the late 1960s, lists the majority of parishioners' addresses being on or near Hogan's Alley, with only a small handful residing on Nanaimo Street. As Leonard Marsh observed in the 1950s, "Many of them could afford to live elsewhere, but it is too obvious that they would not be welcome."[78] Although Marsh's report was written over thirty years after Serafim's death, the entrenched settlement of the area suggests that racist attitudes and beliefs held by white Vancouver settlers had been held for quite some time, leading to communities gathering where they felt comfortable and also safe. To me, the absence of racialized communities at Íỳel̓shn signifies the presence of segregation, with Serafim at the centre of it all as a Black man.

But the contradictions do not end there.

Serafim's physical proximity to whites, particularly white women, had to be even more calculated in the water, where at the turn of the century, racial segregation and gender binaries in swimming spaces were even more strongly enforced than on land.

["Video posted on social media shows a Halifax police officer pointing a gun at the man, who has his hands in the air and is walking away."[79]]

At this time, the Woman's Christian Temperance Union had a firm stronghold on setting the norms of behaviour in so-called Vancouver, creating rules in every aspect of society, including how men and women should visit the beach and how they should dress while visiting. As a Black man and lifeguard, Serafim played a large role in maintaining these rigid gender binaries at the beach and in policing proper beach attire at English Bay. Any deviation from these rigid rules was deeply frowned upon, as evidenced by the English Bay scandal that was the talk of all Vancouver for weeks. As city archivist James Skitt Matthews describes,

> when old Joe Fortes was first self-appointed beach guard here at English Bay, there was a huge boulder at the foot of Denman Street—big as a house—and all women bathed to the west of it and all men to the east. Woe betide any smart-alex [sic] man who intruded westwards. The women called, Joe came running and chased the intruder away.
>
> But, as time went on, women became bolder and invaded the men's part, but still retained their old style bathing suits, which were more like dresses with flounces around the middle hanging like mudguards on a motor car. It was a wonder they were not drowned. They also wore stockings and sandals; they looked very nice, too.

> Then one day one impertinent hussy, bolder than the others, went in bathing without her stockings. She was a sight to behold—she was bare naked right up to her knees. The Woman's Christian Temperance Union wrote to the press about it and what they wrote about the bold woman was published in the newspapers. She sued the W.C.T.U. for libel. The case went to court and she got damages.[80]

Every single one of Serafim's actions had to be calculated, as he was possibly the only Black person in Vancouver allowed to share beach space with whites at this time and the only man on the beach allowed to make physical contact with women.

["The man has his hands raised high in the air, and takes slow, careful steps around the truck, while the officer follows."[81]]

As a swimming instructor, Serafim had to be hyperaware of where his hands were placed, not only because he was subverting segregated gender spaces by teaching women how to swim, but because he was a Black man teaching white women how to swim. In another article about the English Bay scandal, the same woman is once again shamed for her swimming attire and physical proximity to Serafim, while Serafim is praised for his calculated and conservative actions.

["Halifax cop remains on paid duty after he was filmed yelling at a Black man 'I will fill you full of f---ing lead' while pointing a gun at him."[82]]

The Woman's Christian Temperance Union wasn't the only group enforcing these strict gender and racial rules. Emily Murphy, eugenicist and suffragette for white women, was gaining popularity at breakneck pace across so-called Canada with her features in *Maclean's* magazine, in which she fuelled the fear of the "dangers" Chinese and Black communities posed

Serafim teaching a white woman how to swim on English Bay Beach. | Stuart Thomson, City of Vancouver Archives AM336-S3-2-: CVA 677-421

to white settlers by corrupting "vulnerable" and morally superior white people. As Murphy wrote,

> when it comes to railway porters—Ah well! There are some we know of personally whose liberty is more attributable to their good luck than their good behaviour ... One can hardly imagine anything more dangerous than a filthy-minded drug-addict in charge of a coach of sleeping people, whatever his colour may be.[83]

Unfortunately, Murphy's white supremacist rhetoric was extremely well received by white Canadians. In fact, she was rewarded for it by being made police magistrate for the City of Edmonton in 1916. Her rhetoric was further backed by the newly formed Canadian chapter of the Ku Klux Klan.

But somehow, none of this rhetoric mattered when it came to Serafim. Once again, he was made the exception when he was officially named special constable of the Vancouver Police Department, formalizing his role as caretaker, swimming instructor, and beach patroller at English Bay Beach. What does it mean to uphold colonial law in a white supremacist society? The same colonial law that violently displaced hundreds of people from Seṅáḵw. The same colonial law barring Black individuals from owning homes in certain neighbourhoods.

With this level of controversy over gender rules for and scrutiny of Black people in public spaces, was Serafim ever able to explore romantic love? It is hard to say, as it appears nothing has been documented about his love life. I find this incredibly odd, given how much of his life was in the ever-watchful public eye. But then again, there are many possible reasons for this, given the conservative society he was surrounded by. One is that as a man of faith, Serafim may have chosen to be celibate. Many Christians believe that one of the ultimate ways to honour God is to dedicate their entire lives to Him and for God to take the place of a spouse (who is straight, cisgender, and of the "opposite sex"). It is known that one of Serafim's few belongings was a weathered Bible that he read every night before going to sleep. He was so devout that even though he was always busy with lessons, lifeguarding, cleaning the beach, or patrolling the shore, he still made time to attend Mass every single Sunday at the Our Lady of the Holy Rosary Cathedral, a French Gothic–style church in the heart of Vancouver that would have taken him forty to sixty minutes to reach on foot. His dedication was such that he had a "usual" spot in the pews. In this light, it is not impossible to conceive of him choosing celibacy as a way to honour God.

It is also possible that Serafim wasn't celibate, but that his love interests had to remain secret, as his every movement and action was scrutinized by settler society. If he had a relationship with a Black woman, he might have kept it private in an act of protection so that the woman did not have to experience the same level of scrutiny that he faced in the public eye. As late as 1948, Vancouver newspapers ran headlines about Black people receiving death threats and having rocks thrown through their windows, simply for existing as a family.[84] This level of violence was not particular to Vancouver but was seen across Canada. Black individuals were forced to live their lives in the public eye as passive, obedient, and morally pure citizens. Researcher Carolyn Whitzman explains that

> to qualify as Good Negro Citizens, they had to be pious, invisible, and impassive in the public sphere, never seen drunk or otherwise behaving in a disreputable manner. They had to maintain their sexual purity before, during, and after marriage, with consequence much more severe than their male counterparts if they strayed ... They had to be continuously stoic in the face of any racist and sexist slurs and the threat and reality of attacks. They were public property to be scrutinized, commented upon, judged, laughed at, and insulted. If they were sexually assaulted by white men, they wouldn't be believed.[85]

If any of Serafim's love interests were white women, they would have had to remain secret out of fear of possible retaliation by white settlers angry about a relationship that broke colour lines. Many racist stereotypes at this time were of Black men "corrupting" white women, sexually assaulting them, or endangering their physical safety in some way. In this time period, it would have been in Serafim's best interests not to pursue a relationship with any white woman, so as to not endanger himself or his liberty. The backlash against mixed-race relationships was not just hypothetical. When Frederick Douglass, one of the most pivotal American Black rights leaders in the era, married white suffragist Helen Pitts, newspapers across the United States published a series of hateful fearmongering articles that raised the profile of eugenics across Canada and the United States. As Whitzman describes,

> this event occasioned a particularly poisonous screed printed in the *Chicago Tribune* and carried in the *Globe* which portrayed itself as an ally to Black Canadians. In it, the "evil effects" of miscegenation were "set forth in vivid colours by a Chicago physician." According to the article, although "Mr. D is but half African, and therefore, as he himself says, not a Negro [that is, he was being classified as 'mulatto']," Douglass's claim that there is "but one race of mankind" was false. Nature herself had "placed a limit to such admixture." Mortuary statistics showed that the "average life of a half breed is but one quarter of their parents."[86]

Furthermore, the proliferation of the US-based KKK into splinter groups in Canada in the 1920s meant that white supremacist ideology was spreading like wildfire and infiltrating every aspect of society. It spread so quickly, in fact, that in 1921, the KKK Grand Wizard was quoted as saying that membership was "increasing at the rate of 5,000 members a week," and that "north of the Mason-Dixon Line," the numbers were growing twice as fast as they were in the South.[87]

It is within this context that Serafim's possible exploration of love and relationships must be understood. As historian Constance Backhouse writes,

> one of the central planks in the KKK platform was the elimination of interracial marriage. Dating and marriage across "racial" lines signified a racial "levelling" that evoked, in the minds of Klan members, images of white female exploitation and the usurpation of white male privilege. The Klan called for legislation to ban mixed-race marriages, such as existed in many American states below the border. The Klan also worked informally in a myriad of other ways to destroy such relationships. To the south, the American KKK threatened, whipped, assaulted, kidnapped, and lynched scores of Black, non-Protestant, and immigrant men who dared to consort with white Protestant women. The members physically and sexually tortured white women who took up with non-white men. In Canada, the "Constitution and Laws of the Invisible Empire" declared it a "major offence" to be "responsible for the polluting of Caucasion [sic] blood through miscegenation or the commission of any act unworthy of a Klansman."[88]

In this light, pursuing a relationship with a woman outside of colour lines would have been life-threatening. But who says that Serafim was heterosexual? Perhaps the reason no woman was ever known to be his love interest or wife was that his sexual orientation had to be kept secret. While queer relationships have always existed, processes of colonization across Turtle Island, South America, Africa, and the Caribbean have demonized, brutalized, and even killed Two-Spirit, queer, and gender diverse people. Fearful of violent repercussions, generations of Two-Spirit, queer, and gender diverse people have had to hide their identity and orientation and seek out places to meet in relative safety, away from prying eyes. Sadly, this is true in many places around the world, including Canada, even to this day. If Serafim did indeed pursue a queer romantic relationship, it would have had to be kept secret. And what better place than where he had the most authority: the English Bay bathhouse. As early as 1492 in Europe, bathhouses were places where gay men went to seek sexual encounters. At the turn of the twentieth century, bathhouses rose to prominence for being covert sites of queer romance on the West Coast of the United States. As historian Allan Bérubé wrote,

> as a result of homosexual stigma, gay men became "sexual outlaws" and were compelled to create sexual spaces in public, such as parks, restrooms, and public libraries, without being noticed ... In San Francisco, the first references to sex between men in the City's Turkish baths began in the 1890s. By the late 1920s and early '30s, a few of these "favorite spots" in San Francisco began to turn into pre-dominantly gay bathhouses."[89]

From the bathhouse at the River Mersey in Liverpool to the English Bay bathhouse, Serafim's job once again put him in proximity to gender-segregated spaces and half-nude men in a society that did not accept homosexuality in any form. Vancouver, due north of San Francisco and on a similar timeline of the settler colonial project as the United States's West Coast, likely also experienced a rise in sexual public spaces for gay men as the city grew, attracting more and more "able-bodied" men to take advantage of the "Last Best West."

In Vancouver, homosexual stigma, combined with the pre-existing disdain for Black and Asian communities, peaked in 1915 with the high-profile case of Naina and Dalip Singh, two Sikh mill workers who were accused of "gross indecency."[90] This blanket term was used by the Canadian government as early as 1890 through to 1969 to describe anything perceived to be homosexual activity, without defining any specific acts. According to spotty court records, the men were accused of offering seventy-five cents to an undercover police officer and chauffeur in exchange for sexual acts at a railyard. In the end, Naina and Dalip Singh's case was deemed inconclusive. Critics also raise that Dalip, who spoke only Punjabi, could not have communicated a sexual exchange with the chauffeur or the police officer, and further, that Naina was likely entrapped, as the charges against him were only pressed after he spoke out against a Sikh informant whom the police had used during the *Komagata Maru* incident, when the Canadian government denied entry to a group of immigrants from India. As researcher Yilong (Louie) Liu contends, "South Asian immigrants became the target of this law due to the hatred that existed in terms of 'racial difference' that . . . also fascinated the white sexual imagination, yet threatened their homophobic self-identity."[91] It is also important to note that, between 1909 and 1929, the vast majority of sodomy cases in Vancouver were against Sikh men.[92] With the disproportionate amount of vitriol and spectacle around the *Rex v. Singh* case, it is not difficult to imagine that, if indeed Serafim was queer, he likely would have hidden or repressed his queerness even further to ensure that, as a Black man, he would not become a greater target for white supremacists in Vancouver.

Because of the significant span of time between Serafim's life and today, as well as the necessity of maintaining secrecy around queer relationships and queer spaces at the time, it is difficult to obtain information about whether or not the English Bay bathhouse might have been a space for male sexual encounters at the turn of the twentieth century. The possibility always exists, however, and it may be archived in the tattered pages of steamy correspondence in an old, forgotten trunk stored in an attic somewhere, or in the dreaming of a queer ancestor in another realm.

A newspaper clipping from the *Vancouver Sun* after Serafim's death. The title is "Servant—Friend—Protector," a telling encapsulation of how Serafim was seen by white settler society. | Ernest LeMessurier, *Vancouver Daily World*, 1922

8 LEGACY

> You live so that you can look everybody in the face,
> and then you will be afraid of nothing.
> —MOTHER OF SERAFIM FORTES[93]

Servant.

A man so loved for being a servant.

A city mourned for losing a servant.

A city mourned for losing a man who acquiesced to all requests and would no longer be able to fulfill them from his grave.

After losing a servant, the city shifted to remembering it had lost a friend.

And then it remembered that it had also lost a protector. A protector of colonized beaches, a protector of white children, gender binaries, and the status quo.

Which role did the city mourn the most?

Would you mourn a dear friend by memorializing them as your servant?

The fact that the leading newspaper in Vancouver chose *servant* as the first word to honour him with speaks volumes to the white supremacist narrative of Black as slave and Black, perpetually, as servant. While *friend* is included in the tribute, let it be clear that, in the white settler psyche, friendship came second.

The ways we remember a public figure after their passing often reveal that individual's most significant achievements and contributions to society. Whom we choose to memorialize and how we do so also reveal a part of ourselves. To Vancouver, Serafim was a servant first.

Two days after his death, the City of Vancouver honoured Serafim's life by holding a municipal funeral, organized by the chief of police at the time, James Anderson.[94] This type of ceremony was usually reserved for high-profile politicians. Aldermen, priests, schoolchildren, and swimming aficionados, the vast majority of them white, were among the thousands who took to the streets to pay respects to the man who had sacrificed so much for so many. Pulled behind the horse-drawn hearse, Serafim's rescue rowboat was lined with a bounty of magnificent flowers as his spirit left the earthly plane.

The procession wove through Dunsmuir and Granville Streets before finally arriving at the Our Lady of the Holy Rosary Cathedral, Serafim's favourite place of worship. His casket was carried into the crowded church by members of the Vancouver Police Department and met with the profound grieving silence of the congregation, which spilled out into the street.

As a tribute to Serafim's life, Vancouverites raised their voices to sing "Old Black Joe," a tribute song by American Stephen Foster, written to honour enslaved Black communities in the United States.[95]

Gone are the days when my heart was young and gay,
Gone are my friends from the cotton fields away,
Gone from the earth to a better land I know,
I hear their gentle voices calling "Old Black Joe."

I'm coming, I'm coming, for my head is bending low:
I hear those gentle voices calling, "Old Black Joe."[96]

But Serafim was not enslaved. Nor was he from the United States. Nevertheless, the city mourned him as if he were, conflating his gentle nature with servanthood and enslavement.

[In one white imagining, Serafim's ghostly figure is leaning against his old cabin, and on this day "his dusky fingers beat a gentle tattoo on the porch railing, as he hummed a bit of an old song reminiscently. The action, and the peculiar swing and rhyme which he instilled into the quaint tune took me back to the visions of the plantations of the South, the tinkle of the banjo and the sweet, weird harmony of Negro voices singing as they alone can sing."[97]]

The police officers preparing his service disregarded any other songs that could have been chosen to honour him as a person, outside of his race or occupation, as is often done when someone passes. Given that his name was Serafim, meaning "angel," they could have chosen from a wide array of songs that drew upon the imagery of angels. Perhaps he had a favourite song of the era that could have been sung. Seeing as Serafim had attended Mass on a weekly basis, it's likely he had favourite hymns that could have been chosen instead, had anyone taken the opportunity to spend time with him outside of his service role and get to know his favourite hymns. But no such thing happened, and he was forever enshrined as servant of the cotton field, Old Black Joe.

Serafim's decline in health had been noticed for a couple years before his death, beginning with a series of bad colds after performing two deep-water rescues in the middle of winter that left him noticeably reduced in vigour and strength. By 1921, his need for a mobility aid to steady his gait became more pronounced, prompting the City of Vancouver to gift him a cane. In 1922, his health took a turn for the worse: he developed pneumonia, leaving him hospitalized. Long-time family friends Goldvine Howard and her mother, Cassie, immediately visited his bedside, keeping him comfortable and singing to him to keep his spirits up. Vancouver residents brought flowers, and newspapers across the province began to chronicle his death foretold. Here, an inevitable question surfaced: whom to contact to break the news that he was nearing the end of his life?

I can imagine the crushing silence in the room as Serafim searched for an answer.

There's nothing left for me in Trinidad. Who would remember me in Liverpool? My sister in Toronto finna know through the papers—nah bother she. My brother? Quién soy yo al lado de el? Mis padres ya fallecieron, y pronto los iré a encontrar ...

En el nombre del Padre, del Hijo, y del Espíritu Santo ...

Serafim declined offers to make contact with any family. In an article, Goldvine Howard disclosed that Serafim had once confided in her grandmother, Martha Scurry, that he felt he was living in his brother's shadow. His brother had studied medicine and gone on to be a doctor in England. "His family would think, 'What's a lifeguard?' He was obviously not the clever favourite son."[98] Perhaps this admission, as small as it seems to be on the surface, explains why Serafim spent his entire life abroad and never returned home to Trinidad. His Illuminated Address, his countless accolades, and his gold watch—none of it mattered. It would never be enough for *them*. The pain of being rejected by his family, never feeling loved for who he was or who he came to be, must have been a wound so deep that he carried the scar forever.

On February 4, 1922, his spirit journeyed home.

[Amén]

Serafim's funeral was one of the most well attended of the century in Vancouver. News outlets across the province scrambled to publish the news of his passing. Two days after Serafim's death, the *Vancouver Daily Province* wrote:

> It was never suggested to his disadvantage that this is a white man's country. If he had lived beyond the period of useful activity the city would have

> maintained him in comfort. He was able to say that he gave more than value in service for all that he received.[99]

Although it appears that the *Daily Province* intended a dedication to honour Serafim's life, what was written was riddled with racist and ableist remarks. The writers assured their readership that the love Vancouverites had for Serafim would have translated into care for him even after his retirement as a city employee. However, the term *retirement* is not used, but rather exchanged for "beyond the period of useful activity," reminiscent of the language in Slave Codes, wherein enslaved Black people worked until they were severely disabled or no longer "useful." This is deeply connected to the ableism enmeshed within capitalist systems, in which the worker is valued only for as long as they can generate profit for the master, factory owner, or corporation, with the brutal impact that the toll of hard labour on the body, year after year, often robs the worker of their vitality. Had Serafim been granted a home and a higher wage earlier in his life instead of having to constantly prove his worth, perhaps he wouldn't have had to work as arduously as he did, to the detriment of his health. Had he been given adequate rest time during his "live-in" shifts at English Bay and days off throughout his lifeguarding career, his lifespan would have likely extended far longer than it did.

[I can't help but think about my mother's aching knees, bone wearing on bone after years of overtime shifts at the hotel she gave thirty-seven years of her life to. On her days off, early-morning adventures to collect cans from park bins so that she and I could have a special meal at the golden arches. Bosses ripping up medical notes describing my scarred lungs after pneumonia and asserting the need for my mother to stay by my side or face the loss of her daughter. Her exhausted body commanding her to sleep as she did her best to play dolls with me. Surgeries needed far too early, and one cheap nickel pin with "35" in cursive to honour the life force exchanged for decades of

minimum wage and humiliation. Her vital body traded in for a pin beyond her period of useful activity.]

These shortcomings in Serafim's care seemed to be dismissed as the *Daily Province* also assured their readership that the city's love for Serafim transcended race, despite their open use of white supremacist rhetoric. By utilizing the term *white man's country*, a slogan that had been used to elect city aldermen in 1907 and to maintain whites in positions of power in Vancouver, in a tribute to Serafim, while simultaneously claiming that nobody would ever have said this to him, "to his disadvantage," the writer reveals that he is indeed aware of white supremacy and its impact on people "like Joe" but defends that there are exceptions whenever deemed appropriate by white society, further bolstering the white supremacist hegemony and minimizing the scale of violence across society.

In another article "honouring" his life, a writer for the *Vancouver Sun* relayed,

> an old coloured man lies in a Vancouver Morgue, and every child, every man and every woman find time, from their work or play, to be sorry ... it is not hard to write the obituary of statesmen, politicians, or great artists. Their work is tangible. The milestones which mark their progress are engraven with letters that he who runs may read. But this coloured man never wrote a book, never saved his country, never marched in a parade, nor condescended magnificently to tell the press that Vancouver had a great future. Just the same, Vancouver is mourning him more sincerely than it probably would great statesmen, politicians, or artists.[100]

Even in a dedication intended to honour the life of Serafim, the writer can't help but bring up what are perceived as Serafim's shortcomings in the same breath as praising his achievements. In fact, the dedication appears to be more of a shocked observation about how the city's residents were mourning the death of an uneducated Black man to the same extent as educated white politicians and public servants.

In the days after his death, newspapers across the province featured poems by readers dedicated to Serafim, bidding him farewell. Many riffed on "Old Black Joe," highlighting his Blackness and his servanthood. Others, in stark contrast, again attempted to erase his Blackness while preserving other aspects of his character that settlers attributed to whiteness and glorifying it. "Whitest soul that ever nature framed in Black," ended one poem, while another by a reader in Kamloops read,

> The sun may shine as brightly yet,
> The skies may hold its azure tone.
> Another may fill old Joe's "place"
> But none who "knew" can e'er forget
> That Joe lived for his bairns
> alone
> and loved them all. his own "white race"
> a whiter man can not be met—
> Than poor Old Joe.[101]

On the day of his passing, Goldvine Howard and her grandmother, Martha Scurry, crossed the city to Serafim's cabin at Ííyel̓shn to retrieve the waistcoat that he had left to her. The little cabin overlooking the inlet, where she and her family had shared so many memories with Serafim, now so empty and devoid of meaning without him there.

And devoid of his waistcoat too.

Serafim's beloved waistcoat, into which he had secretly sewn all of his earnings to gift to Goldvine's mother, Cassie, disappeared on the day of his death before Goldvine and Martha had a chance to retrieve it. To this day, neither his waistcoat nor his life earnings have been recovered, begging a larger question: who was so callously motivated to raid Serafim's cabin on the day of his death for his life savings? Two months after Serafim's death, an article in the *Vancouver Sun* confirmed that a court official had conducted a careful search of the former residence, assessing Serafim's personal effects at a value of only $228.65.[†102] No cash or will was found in his cabin.

Serafim's cabin was passed on to D. Saggers, an "old employee" of the Park board.[103] Saggers, however, was not required to be on duty year-round, once again highlighting the disparity between the expectations on Serafim and on white city employees.[104] Alec McLean, a white "old waterman," was appointed as Serafim's successor by the end of July 1922, with the *Vancouver Daily Province* noting that "Alec has personality" and that with time he would be just as popular as Joe among Vancouver residents.[105]

Years later, Serafim's creeper-clad cabin, pretty little garden and all, was demolished, along with the other cottages in the area that once lined the beachfront. Today, the spot where Serafim's home stood is surrounded by towering skyscrapers and a grove of six elm trees and is marked by a plaque dedicated to a Vancouver Park Board commissioner. There is no indication that Serafim ever lived there.

Despite the contradictions of dedications that both insulted and elevated Serafim's life, it is striking that, even more than a hundred years later, his memory has not been lost to time.

Five years after Serafim's death, in 1927, people of all ages, races, and class backgrounds emptied their pockets to fundraise for a memorial fountain in his honour. The granite drinking fountain with bronze cast is just steps away from the site of his former cabin and features his image in a circular frame, with three small children playing in the water below. The fountain still stands to this day.

Fifty-four years after Serafim's death, in 1976, the Vancouver Public Library named its branch in the West End neighbourhood where he had once lived the Joe Fortes Branch.

† $4,000 CAD in 2024

The author under elm trees. | Photo by Keith William Miller

Memorial plaque for George Wainborn at the former site of Serafim's cabin. | Photo by Ruby Smith Díaz

Sixty-three years after his death, in 1985, a high-end restaurant named their establishment Joe Fortes Seafood & Chop House in his honour.†

In 1986, over sixty years after his death, Serafim was named "Vancouver Citizen of the Century" by the Vancouver Historical Society, and in 2002, the National Film Board of Canada released an animated short about his life, created by Jill Haras. In the short, *Joe*, Haras illustrates Serafim's warm and lively personality and the struggles that he endured facing anti-Black racism, summarized by an incident in which an old white woman yells to her younger relative to not touch or engage with him. The film's description asserts that, "through his determination, kindness and love for children, Joe helped shift attitudes,"[106] without explicitly naming the systemic racism he endured from white Vancouverites or the fact that this was not work he had set out to do. While the film is an homage to Serafim's life, it is a disservice to him not to name the systemic and interpersonal racism he faced and to summarize these aggressions as "attitudes" that he "helped shift," as though he himself were responsible for the racism he encountered in the first place.

In 2013, as part of Black History Month, Canada Post released a stamp honouring Serafim's legacy: a black-and-white image of a smiling Serafim in his swimsuit against a colourized image of Íỷel̓shn in the background. "My overall intention, explains [artist Lara] Minja, was to bring life to the character of Joe Fortes, showing him as a strong and personable man, who was caring, responsible, fun-loving, and honourable."[107]

In 2020, Vancouver artists Carson Ting and Annie Chen created a mural honouring Serafim in the West End, as part of the Vancouver Mural Festival. Serafim is drawn in a whimsical cartoon style in blue hues, sporting a red top that reads "Joe" as he leaps across an array of geometric shapes. The artists state, "The West End is a wonderfully rich

† Ironically, the restaurant that is named after him wouldn't have been a place where he could afford to eat, with most menu items averaging thirty dollars and catering to a "high-end" crowd looking for a fine dining experience. Little else about the restaurant connects to Serafim besides reference to his "warm" nature and his "character and personality," which the restaurant aims to recreate in its atmosphere. With the single-dimensional profile and stylized line drawing of Serafim on the restaurant's menus, he once again becomes a mascot.

and friendly community home to residents of all cultures, backgrounds, and professions—we hope to represent and bright up our neighbourhood through colour and fun imagery in this mural."[108]

Now, in the twenty-first century, Serafim is remembered as an "unlikely" hero.[109] This description begs the question, which traits are most likely to make someone a hero? It could be argued that all heroes are unlikely, in the sense that it's improbable any child is raised by their parents and guardians to grow up with the purpose of becoming a hero, regardless of their gender, racial identity, or socio-economic status. So which identity markers make someone less likely to be considered a hero? Class? Stature? Race? Serafim Fortes is an "unlikely" hero because he was a poor man of African and Spanish descent who managed to gain the respect and trust of white people in a time when whites actively set laws and policies to exclude non-whites from Vancouver society and to threaten their very existence. He became a hero to whites because he survived the barriers that they themselves placed against people like him. This is an uncomfortable truth that most would prefer to ignore or forget.

Grief can provide an opportunity for loved ones and community to formulate their own legacy. It can allow for the immortalizing of their relationship to the deceased in whichever way they see fit, even if it is inaccurate, because the deceased is not present to provide correction or to voice how they would like to be remembered. I believe this was the case for Vancouver in relation to Serafim Fortes; there was a convenient forgetting of the cotton hook in his cheek, of racist slurs in bars and at the beach, of labour underpaid by city institutions, and of the very city that claimed to love him hosting the KKK. There was a reinvention of how white Vancouver related to Serafim: as an equal, as a "Black-skinned old lifeguard with a white soul."[110] No longer Serafim, but our servant and friend, Joe.

There are so many aspects of his story that I wish I could know. I often wonder, what might he have said to me, an Afro Latina, that he might not have shared with a white reporter? What language would he have spoken to me in? What are the stories that *he* would have wished to be remembered by? I dream of a day when I might find, somewhere in Vancouver, Serafim's "little book," discarded and covered in a layer of dust, on some garage sale table, filled with notes in Spanish and Patois. I dream of the day I might get to know him in his own words.

Until then, his story, or the absence of his story in his own words, reminds me of the critical importance of telling my life in my own words, on my own terms. I owe it to my ancestors. I owe it to so many like Serafim who have had their histories altered and even erased to appease settler colonial narratives. I owe it to myself.

9

SOLILOQUY FOR SERAFIM

Your ship, destined to take you back to the warm Caribbean ocean,
is battered in a storm and damaged beyond repair.

You end up nestled between mountains and ocean, homelands of the
Musqueam, Squamish, and the Tsleil-Waututh.

The temperatures here hover around twelve degrees most of the year.
Cattle horn never too heavy for him to carry …

You shiver as you look up at the Two Sisters, comforted by their
presence,
longing for the sound of kaiso on your ear
and the taste of buss up and ackee on your tongue.
You are nineteen years old.

Somewhere along the way you find a rowboat.
You paddle up to where there is soft footing. Íy̓el̓shn.

Across the water, Sen̓áḵw, where the Squamish people have come every
summer since time immemorial.

The water is *nice*. You drink half a cup of it every day to keep good.
A canvas tent will make shelter. New friends will come by with chairs,
a table, a silver teapot.

You dive in the ocean waters, your strong arms reminiscing with the feeling of weightlessness half a world away.

Sunset after sunset, you serve drinks, and clean up the trash left behind on the sandy shore.

You soon learn that not every man knows how to swim in deep waters,
so you take it upon yourself to be of service.
You learn that just ten years before your arrival, Seṅáḵw became a place
your friends were confined to.
Government man seh that the city needs to grow
He draws a reserve—
a line on the sand
"We were never here for winters"
a line that shan't be passed.
Still, the nation goes on, ten thousand years strong.
Still, a home.

You imagine yourself one day in a home,
like the ones of those helping themselves to land,
with white picket fences, wide cedar planks, and windows.

Over tea, you hear whispers that no Asiatic, Negro, or Indian can own a home.

—Payshent man ride danki—

You let your foot sink into the sand and let the ocean wash over you
once again.

To keep strong,
you swim every morning
and look across to Seṅáḵw's shore.
Like ritual,
women with woven cedar hats gather clams and crabs along
her shore, keeping time with daybreak.
Strong men paddle in long dugout canoes with brightly painted sides,
keeping watch on the inlet.

Give thanks to the land fi providing.

Granville doubles in size,
Íỷel̓shn swells with new visitors,
all eager to breathe the clear(ed) ocean air.
Beyond the hazy horizon, smoky remnants of giant cedars.
In shallow waters you teach the city how to swim—

"Kick your feet,
don't stop kicking your feet."

Your presence punctuates the shoreline,
protects the peace of segregation.

"Old Black Joe"
"Dusky Joe"
"Portuguese Joe"
"Cotton-Eye Joe"
"Light-Skinned Joe"
"N----- Joe"
"Seraphim Joe"

The government man seh
it is your beach to take care of now—
gifts you a shining new constable badge.
Soon after, one likkle house.
At last, four wooden walls!
No longer will the canvas pronounce the sigh of the northern wind.
At night, alone, you clasp your hands together,
give thanks fi putting a roof over your head
and food fi eat.
Glory be to God,
for he has allowed you to touch white flowers in the ocean
and not be maimed.
Glory be to God
for sparing you the fate of Emmett Till;
perhaps the loneliness is worth your safety.

One morning,
barges, like the one that failed your journey, arrive at Seṅáḵw.
The government man seh that the city needs to grow.
Sacred fires quenched,
longhouses emptied,
ceremony frozen in time,
a nation of people forced onto barge deck,
stolen from her shore.

The ocean swallows tears, grieves in salt.

Seṅá<u>k</u>w is empty.

You make Great Britain proud,
keeping ruckus off the beach!
Now, fi two dolla a day you guard Íy̓əl̓shn—
soft footing for whites from the upper echelons of society.
White sand sparkles with broken glass
you clean up just so
fi live another day.
Nearby, Chinese men carry loaded rifles,
guard children, homes, and storefronts
from whites from the upper echelons of society
expressing their raging desire for a white Canada.
Cobblestone sparkles with broken glass.
All skin teeth eh laugh,
Clean up just so
fi live another day.
Your body aches,
joints stiffen, protesting having to part Pacific waters as daily ritual.
Ten years have passed now.
You make do with what the growing city pay you.
If Jesus turned one fish fi plenty.
You can make three month pay last the year
No matter how rough the water, the children always put a smile pon
your face.

Hazlo por ellos, Serafim. Do it for them.

Six elm trees protect your rooftop,
but they can't stop the cold fi reach under the door.
One night, through the chattering of your teeth and the ruthless rain,
you hear the inlet scream—
can it be?

—Nuh trouble me so—

Pull the sheets up. Rub your arms briskly to create heat. Curl your foot in tight.
Soon come morning, just get through this autumn night.

The inlet screams again.

No puede ser.

You know that cry too well …
That sound is not of the inlet screaming,
it is the scream of a life about to be taken by the sea.

A jolt runs through your body.
You leap up, abandon frigid sheets,
throwing on your damp waistcoat as you run out your cabin door.

"You must go, Serafim!
Get in the boat,
there is no time to waste,

nuh think about the cold!"

Unlike the others
with "darker colouration,"

you split the inlet bed with your paddle,
ask the moon to interrupt Vantablack,
and light your way.
The ocean reveals two men
clinging to wood and barnacle,
doing their best to not be sacrificed by the waves they claim to conquer.
Your mighty wing scoops them up
into your small lifeboat—

saved by the Negro Joe!
Forever grateful to you,
who has saved them from a watery grave!

Forever grateful to you,
they disappear into the dead of night,
back into their fire-warmed homes, surrounded by their families.

The newspapers may sing your praise come tomorrow,
but tonight
you hang your drenched clothes,
ignore the cold lodged deeper now in your bones,
remembering that with every life saved, you earn your existence.

The next morning, the sunrise awakens Íỷeỉshn,
but for the first time in thirty years, you are not there to greet her.

Your body won't let you—
"Get up, Joe!"
There is trash to clean off the beach,
a badge to live up to.
Who will watch over your beach?

Nightfall envelopes Íy̓el̓shn, and you are not there to greet her.
Your body won't let you,
not tomorrow,
nor the day after.
Grandmothers, prostitutes, burglars,
children, white supremacists, Sunday school priests—
all saved by you—
hold their breath collectively
to see their Serafim rise again.

Days pass,
the sun peers over the snow-capped mountains.
Today, Serafim, you rise again.

The city exclaims your name from rooftops,
Vancouver children breathe a sigh of relief—their friend is back!
How you have weathered the storm!

A gifted cane with your name on it now eases your lumbering pace.
A gold watch from your friends with your name inscribed

reminds you of the inexorable passage of time.

One day you take ill.
Your body sick.
Lungs once buoying you in ocean water let water in.
You ache for the Caribbean sun to warm your mahogany skin,
and fi kaiso music to soothe your bones.
Children gather around your bed, vigilant for any sign of healing,

You smile at them and ignore the warnings of their light skin and your dark skin
holding each other in peace.

There is no letter to send,
nobody left to write home to.

In the night
your spirit soars over the Two Sisters,
and somewhere in Trinidad a griot announces your death.

"Although he was born of alien race
although he was born of alien colour
although he was a darkie
although he was black outside,
he was white all through.
He was OUR *Joe,*
our friend Joe."

His name was Serafim Joseph Fortes,
forever at Íy̓el̓shn's shore.

Señor Fortes, for you,
the ocean swallows tears, grieves in salt.

So it go.

ACKNOWLEDGMENTS

This book was written on the unceded and stolen territories of the Musqueam, Squamish, and Tsleil-Waututh peoples, with later portions written on the unceded and stolen territories of the Stz'uminus peoples. I lift my hands up in utmost gratitude to the peoples and lands of these nations that have been here since time immemorial.

I wish to acknowledge that the later portions of the book were written during the active genocide of the Palestinian people, with a current estimated death toll of at least 100,000—many of their bodies will never be recovered. As South African president and activist Nelson Mandela once said, "But we know too well that our freedom is incomplete without the freedom of Palestinians." My freedom as of now is incomplete.

I urge everyone to take action and learn about the Boycott, Divestment, Sanctions (BDS) movement at bdsmovement.net. If my book was purchased at a retailer on the BDS list, please consider donating to the Palestine Children's Relief Fund (pcrf.net) and learning more at the Palestinian human rights organization Al-Haq (alhaq.org).

Searching for Serafim would not have been possible without the generosity and support of the following individuals:

My partner, Keith, thank you for being my biggest cheerleader in every aspect of my life and for supporting this dream from its very inception until the end and beyond. I'm eternally grateful for the multitude of ways you have supported my person and my artistry. Thank you for being the best partner I could ever ask for.

Amy George (Ta'ah), thank you for opening up your home to me when I first arrived on your territories. Thank you for your warmth, thank you for sharing with me so much of your life experience and for sharing with me the histories of your territory and your people.

Anam Ahmed, thank you for helping to shape my work in the beginning stages during my BIPOC Writers Mentorship at ECW Press.

The Arsenal Pulp team: MASSIVE THANK YOU! Especially Brian, Catharine, and JC for believing in this book and uplifting my work. Jazmin and Rebecca, your cover art brought my words to life beyond my wildest imaginings. I am forever grateful to you all.

Brian and Naava, for your generous support in helping me navigate databases and historical newspapers.

Harsha Walia, for your immense generosity in reading my work over and over again and helping me to make even more connections to other struggles of racialized peoples in so-called Canada and for all your work that I have learned from that moves toward decolonization, land back, and collective liberation.

Hari Alluri, for your constant encouragement to write poetry since I was twenty-one years old, for mentoring me through those formative years, and for seeing my potential even when I couldn't.

James Dempsey (QEPD), my first Native Studies professor, to whom I owe so much of my knowledge about Turtle Island and all the injustices that have happened on these lands. Thank you.

Dawn, Marianna, Nassim, Paola, and West, thank you for being the absolute best hype team I could ever ask for and for believing in me and my work in moments when the going got rough.

"Soliloquy for Serafim" was originally written and recorded as an audio output during my WEDGE Residency with the Contemporary Art Gallery of Vancouver and Ground Floor, with the mentorship support of Wayde Compton. Thank you all for providing the creative space, resources, and support during my residency to research the life of Serafim, Brown Skin Beach, and the history of Sen̓áḵw and Íy̓elshn.

Wayde Compton, thank you for encouraging me to write this time and time again. Without your encouragement, "Soliloquy for Serafim" would have been the only piece I ever created, and my research on and obsession with these topics would have remained a constellation of thoughts locked away in my mind.

De todo corazón, gracias a todes.

NOTES

INTRODUCTION

1 Lisa Anne Smith and Barbara Rogers, *Our Friend Joe: The Joe Fortes Story* (Vancouver: Ronsdale Press, 2012), 28.

CHAPTER 1: QUERENCIA

2 "The Banana Boat Song," a traditional Jamaican folk song made famous by Harry Belafonte's 1956 version.

3 vanbuekl, "Concerted National Action Overdue for All the Children Who Never Came Home from Residential Schools," National Centre for Truth and Reconciliation, June 2, 2021, https://nctr.ca/concerted-national-action-overdue-for-all-the-children-who-never-came-home-from-residential-schools/.

CHAPTER 2: HE ALWAYS FOLLOWED THE SEA

4 Goldvine Howard, "Joe Fortes of English Bay," *British Columbia Historical News* 24, no. 4 (1991): 16–18.

5 *The Current with Matt Galloway*, "The Excavation of WH," produced by Alisa Siegel, aired May 31, 2023, on CBC Radio, https://www.cbc.ca/radio/thecurrent/wednesday-may-31-2023-episode-transcript-1.6861288.

6 *The Current with Matt Galloway*, "The Excavation of WH."

7 "Occupations," Statistics Canada, updated April 1, 2008, https://www65.statcan.gc.ca/acyb01/acyb01_0003-eng.htm.

8 *Sold Into Slavery* (Port of Spain: National Archives of Trinidad and Tobago, n.d.), https://www.natt.gov.tt/sites/default/files/pdfs/Emancipation_-_SOLD_INTO_SLAVERY.pdf.

9 *The Current with Matt Galloway*, "The Excavation of WH."

10 Ben Johnson, "Liverpool," Historic UK, December 28, 2015, https://www.historic-uk.com/HistoryMagazine/DestinationsUK/Liverpool/.

11 Noel Robinson, "Joe Fortes, Children's Friend," *Vancouver Daily World*, February 6, 1922.

12 William Miller, "The *Robert Kerr* (1866–1911)," The Nauticapedia, accessed June 26, 2024, https://www.nauticapedia.ca/Gallery/Robert_Kerr_logs.php.

13 Charles Rusnell and Jennie Russell, "Black Grande Prairie Doctor Testifies He Felt Threatened by Noose Tied by White Colleague," CBC News, June 14, 2021, https://www.cbc.ca/news/canada/edmonton/black-grande-prairie-doctor-testifies-he-felt-threatened-by-noose-tied-by-white-colleague-1.6065691.

14 Jayne Triber, "Slavery and Law in 17th Century Massachusetts," National Park Service, accessed August 12, 2024, https://www.nps.gov/articles/000/slavery-and-law-in-early-ma.htm.

15 "On This Day—Mar 06, 1857: Dred Scott," Equal Justice Initiative, accessed June 24, 2024, https://calendar.eji.org/racial-injustice/mar/06.

16 Rusnell and Russell, "Black Grande Prairie Doctor."

17 Rusnell and Russell, "Black Grande Prairie Doctor."

18 *The Current with Matt Galloway*, "The Excavation of WH."

19 Katie Hyslop, "How a Black Student Paid the Price for Racism at a Vancouver School," *The Tyee*, September 11, 2019, https://thetyee.ca/News/2019/09/11/Vancouver-School-Racist-Video/.

CHAPTER 3: ALL CRAB FIND DEY HOLE

20 Miller, "The *Robert Kerr* (1866–1911)."

21 Olivia Stefanovich, "Sinixt Indigenous Nation Not 'Extinct' in Canada, Supreme Court Rules," CBC News, April 23, 2021, https://www.cbc.ca/news/politics/supreme-court-of-canada-desautel-sinixt-ruling-1.5998062.

22 James Skitt Matthews, *Early Vancouver, Vol. 4* (Vancouver: City of Vancouver, [1944] 2011), 24.

23 City of Vancouver, "Discriminatory Covenants, Language and Encumbrances on Vancouver Land Titles," motion from Councillor Sarah Kirby-Yung, February 2020, https://council.vancouver.ca/20200225/documents/motionb13.pdf.

24 "Joe Fortes of English Bay Ain' Noway Pahticlah 'Bout a Write-Up," *Vancouver Daily Province*, December 10, 1910.

25 Smith and Rogers, *Our Friend Joe*, 70.

26 James Skitt Matthews, *Early Vancouver, Vol. 7* (Vancouver: City of Vancouver, [1956] 2011), 127–128.

27 From Awakening the Canoes Ceremony held at Whey-ah-Wichen in resistance to Kinder Morgan on May 4, 2022, transcribed by the author.

28 Oral history recounted by səlilwətaɬ Nation Elder Amy George (Ta'ah) and transcribed by the author.

29 "Residential School History," National Centre for Truth and Reconciliation, accessed August 12, 2024, https://nctr.ca/education/teaching-resources/residential-school-history/.

30 Matthews, *Early Vancouver, Vol. 7*, 125.

31 Leslie Marmon Silko, "Long Time Ago," in *Storyteller* (New York: Penguin Publishing Group, 2012; originally published in 1981 by Seaver Books), 125–126.

32 James W. St.G. Walker, *The Black Loyalists: The Search for a Promised Land in Nova Scotia and Sierra Leone, 1783–1870* (Toronto: University of Toronto Press, 1992), 28.

33 "Who Was 'Gassy Jack' and Why Was His Statue Toppled in Vancouver?" *National Post*, February 15, 2022, https://nationalpost.com/news/canada/who-was-gassy-jack-and-why-was-his-statue-toppled-in-vancouver.

34 Wayde Compton, "Hogan's Alley," *The Canadian Encyclopedia*, updated February 14, 2019, https://www.thecanadianencyclopedia.ca/en/article/hogans-alley.

35 Joyce Berry, *Childhood Days*, short film, posted by vancouverstories125, September 28, 2011, 2:31, https://www.youtube.com/watch?v=sxiYACJQFlo; Colleen Addison, "Dressed in Black: From Africa to Canada," *The Source*, accessed August 12, 2024, https://thelasource.com/en/2020/02/17/dressed-in-black-from-africa-to-canada/.

36 "Council and the Board," *The Province*, April 16, 1901.

37 Andrew Farris, "The Lifeguard Joe Fortes," On This Spot, accessed June 27, 2024, https://onthisspot.ca/cities/vancouver/joefortes.

38 "Honoring Black History in Parks," City of Vancouver, accessed June 27, 2024, https://vancouver.ca/people-programs/honoring-black-history-in-parks.aspx.

39 Isabelle Raghem, "'Systemic Racism, Prejudice': 50 Years Later VPD's First Black Officer Reflects What's Changed, Hasn't," *CityNews Vancouver*, June 4, 2020, https://vancouver.citynews.ca/2020/06/04/first-black-officer-vancouver-on-protests/.

40 Angela Sterritt, "The Little-Known History of Squamish Nation Land in Vancouver," CBC News, April 21, 2019, https://www.cbc.ca/news/canada/british-columbia/little-known-history-of-squamish-nation-land-in-vancouver-1.5104584.

41 Maria Wallstam and Nathan Crompton, "City of Perpetual Displacement: 100 Years Since the Destruction of the Kitsilano Reserve," *The Mainlander*, July 25, 2013, https://themainlander.com/2013/07/25/city-of-perpetual-displacement-100-years-since-the-destruction-of-the-kitsilano-reserve/.

42 Silko, "Long Time Ago," 128–129.

CHAPTER 4: READING BETWEEN THE LINES OF WHITE SUPREMACY

43 Nya Lewis (curator), *An Insufficient Record: The Photo Ethics of Preserving Black Vancouver*, Grunt Gallery, exhibited May 20–June 18, 2022, accessed June 27, 2024, https://grunt.ca/exhibitions/an-insufficient-record/.

44 Lani Russwurm, "Black History Month: The Remarkable Scurry Family," Forbidden Vancouver Walking Tours, March 18, 2021, https://forbiddenvancouver.ca/blog/black-history-month-the-remarkable-scurry-family/.

45 Howard, "Joe Fortes of English Bay."

46 "About *Black in Latin America*," PBS, accessed June 27, 2024, https://www.pbs.org/wnet/black-in-latin-america/about/.

CHAPTER 5: QUANTIFYING MELANIN

47 Wayde Compton, *After Canaan: Essays on Race, Writing, and Region* (Vancouver: Arsenal Pulp Press, 2010), 24.

48 Ethel Wilson, *The Innocent Traveller* (Toronto: New Canadian Library, [1949] 2008), 141.

49 Smith and Rogers, *Our Friend Joe*, 4.

50 "Unveil Bronze Memorial to City's Beloved Life Guard," *Vancouver Daily Province*, June 25, 1927.

51 Peter James Hudson, "The Lost Tribe of a Lost Tribe," in *Black British Columbia and the Politics of Space*, ed. Katherine McKittrick and Clyde Woods (Toronto: Between the Lines, 2007), 159.

52 Justin Parkinson, "The Significance of Sarah Baartman," BBC *News Magazine*, January 7, 2016, https://www.bbc.com/news/magazine-35240987.

53 "Death Calls Joe Fortes, Lifeguard," *Vancouver Sun*, February 5, 1922; "Old Joe Has Passed Away," *Vancouver Daily Province*, February 4, 1922.

54 Robinson, "Joe Fortes, Children's Friend."

55 "At Street Corners," *Vancouver Daily Province*, November 26, 1910.

56 Jacqui Underwood, "Joe Fortes' Illuminated Address," Old Hastings Mill Store Museum, February 3, 2021, https://hastingsmillmuseum.ca/blog/f/joe-fortes-illuminated-address.

CHAPTER 6: JOE FORTES, MODEL NEGRO CITIZEN

57 Jessica Hardy, "The Legacy of Joe Fortes, Vancouver's First Beloved Lifeguard," *Montecristo Magazine*, April 28, 2021, https://montecristomagazine.com/community/joe-fortes-lifeguard; Farris, "The Lifeguard Joe Fortes."

58 "'Joe' Should Get the Medal," *Evening Record* (Windsor), December 7, 1898.

59 "Why They Are All Thankful," *Vancouver Daily Province*, October 14, 1903.

60 "Taxed at Every Turn," *Vancouver Daily Province*, May 22, 1900.

61 Hudson, "The Lost Tribe of a Lost Tribe," 172.

62 "Great Reception for the Big Black," *Vancouver Daily Province*, March 10, 1909.

63 "Jack Johnson (1878–1946)," American Experience, PBS, accessed June 28, 2024, https://www.pbs.org/wgbh/americanexperience/features/fight-jack-johnson-1878-1946/.

64 Roy Brown, "Joe Fortes, English Bay 'Senor' Was Greatly Beloved Figure," *Vancouver Sun*, May 12, 1954.

65 C.L.R. James, "The Economics of Lynching (1940)," in *C.L.R. James on the "Negro Question,"* ed. Scott McLemee (Jackson: University of Mississippi Press, 1996), 34–36.

CHAPTER 7: ON LOVE AND BEING LOVED

66 Matthew McRae, "The Story of the *Komagata Maru*," Canadian Museum for Human Rights, April 28, 2017, https://humanrights.ca/story/story-komagata-maru.

67 Bob Becken, "'Defund the Police' Calls in Canada Began in 2020. Today, Budgets Continue to Climb," CBC News, updated February 12, 2023, https://www.cbc.ca/radio/day6/defund-police-2023-budgets-grow-1.6741711.

68 Elisha Fieldstadt, "Morgan Wallen, Caught Using N-Word, Says He Hasn't 'Thought About' Racism in Country Music," NBC News, July 23, 2021, https://www.nbcnews.com/pop-culture/music/morgan-wallen-caught-using-n-word-says-he-hasn-t-n1274833.

69 bell hooks, *All About Love* (New York: Harper Perennial, 2000), 22.

70 "Indigenous Title and the Doctrine of Discovery," Indigenous Corporate Training Inc., March 30, 2023, https://www.ictinc.ca/blog/indigenous-title-and-the-doctrine-of-discovery.

71 Russwurm, "Black History Month."

72 Howard, "Joe Fortes of English Bay."

73 "A Jolly Evening at the Beach," *Vancouver Daily Province*, September 8, 1900.

74 Robyn Maynard, *Policing Black Lives: State Violence in Canada from Slavery to the Present* (Halifax: Fernwood Publishing, 2017), 25.

75 "Joe Fortes Had a Busy Day," *Vancouver Daily Province*, June 4, 1906.

76 "Prevent Crime Is Mr. Fortes' Motto," *Vancouver Daily Province*, December 30, 1904.

77 "Joe Fortes Had a Busy Day."

78 Compton, "Hogan's Alley."

79 Emily Baron Cadloff, "Cop Who Told Black Man 'I Will Fill You Full of Lead' Under Investigation," *Vice News*, March 31, 2021, https://www.vice.com/en/article/k7a43y/halifax-police-officer-threaten-black-man-gunpoint.

80 Matthews, *Early Vancouver, Vol. 7*, 128.

81 Cadloff, "Cop Who Told Black Man."

82 Cadloff, "Cop Who Told Black Man."

83 Emily F. Murphy, "The Underground System: Some Secrets of the Sale and Distribution of Drugs," *Maclean's* 33, no. 5 (1920): 12.

84 "Young Negro Couple Threatened With Death Unless They Move," unknown newspaper, April 15, 1948, in Lewis, *An Insufficient Record*.

85 Carolyn Whitzman, *Clara at the Door with a Revolver: The Scandalous Black Suspect, the Exemplary White Son, and the Murder That Shocked Toronto* (Vancouver: UBC Press, 2023), 142.

86 Whitzman, *Clara at the Door*, 73–74.

87 William G. Shepherd, "Night Riders Come to Canada," *Maclean's*, October 1921.

88 Constance Backhouse, *Colour-Coded: A Legal History of Racism in Canada, 1900–1950* (Toronto: University of Toronto Press, 1999), 185.

89 Allan Bérubé, "The History of Gay Bathhouses," *Journal of Homosexuality* 44, nos. 3–4 (2003): 33–53.

90 Meera Bains, "Film Exposes Persecution of Sikhs in Early Vancouver, Director Says," CBC News, August 15, 2008, https://www.cbc.ca/news/canada/british-columbia/film-exposes-persecution-of-sikhs-in-early-vancouver-director-says-1.758528.

91 Yilong (Louie) Liu, "Confronting Ambiguity: The Intersection of Racial and Sexual Marginalisation and Repression in *Rex vs Singh* (2008) and *Seeking Single White Male* (2010)" (master's thesis, OCAD University, 2018), https://openresearch.ocadu.ca/id/eprint/2235/1/Liu_Yilong_2018_MA_CADN_MRP.pdf, 12.

92 Ali Kazimi, John Greyson, and Richard Fung, *Rex vs. Singh*, short film, 2008, 29:25. Commissioned by the Queer History Project of Out on Screen, Vancouver Queer Film Festival.

CHAPTER 8: LEGACY

93 "Old-Timer Talk," *Vancouver Daily World*, December 10, 1921.

94 "Entire City Will Pay Its Respects to Warm-Hearted 'Joe' Fortes," *Vancouver Sun*, February 6, 1922.

95 "Great Crowd at Funeral of Joe Fortes," *Vancouver Daily World*, February 7, 1922.

96 Stephen C. Foster, "Old Black Joe," Poetry Foundation, accessed October 4, 2024, https://www.poetryfoundation.org/poems/44257/old-black-joe.

97 "Joe Fortes of English Bay Ain' Noway Pahticlah 'Bout a Write-Up."

98 Howard, "Joe Fortes of English Bay."

99 "Joe Fortes," *Vancouver Daily Province*, February 6, 1922.

100 "Ol' Joe," *Vancouver Sun*, February 6, 1922.

101 "Joe Fortes—Three Tributes," *Vancouver Daily Province*, February 8, 1922.

102 "Joe Fortes' Estate Amounts to $268.65," *Vancouver Sun*, April 28, 1922.

103 "Bathing Beaches to Be Improved," *Vancouver Sun*, February 16, 1922.

104 "Successor to Fortes Not to Be Appointed," *Vancouver Daily World*, February 23, 1922; "Bathing Beaches to Be Improved."

105 "Alec McLean Is Joe's Successor," *Vancouver Daily Province*, July 15, 1922.

106 Jill Haras, *Joe*, short film, NFB/ONF Distribution, 2008, 8:55, https://www.nfb.ca/distribution/film/joe.

107 "Oliver Jones and Joe Fortes," Canada Post, February 1, 2013, https://www.canadapost-postescanada.ca/cpc/en/personal/collectibles/stamp-stories/2013-02-01-oliver-jones-and-joe-fortes.

108 "VMF2020: West End," VMF, accessed August 29, 2024, https://vanmuralfest.ca/blog/westend.

109 "The Lifeguard Joe Fortes: Vancouver's Unlikely Hero," Culture Days, accessed July 15, 2024, https://culturedays.ca/en/events/aff37402-96df-4212-ad9e-40e60f74a3af; Farris, "The Lifeguard Joe Fortes."

110 "Boy 'Chips In' for 'Old Joe,'" *Vancouver Daily Province*, April 6, 1926.

BIBLIOGRAPHY

Compton, Wayde. *After Canaan: Essays on Race, Writing, and Region*. Vancouver: Arsenal Pulp Press, 2010.

Matthews, James Skitt (compiler). *Conversations with Khahtsahlano, 1932–1954*. Vancouver: Talonbooks, 2022, originally published by City of Vancouver Archives in 1955.

Matthews, James Skitt. *Early Vancouver, Vol. 4*. Vancouver: City of Vancouver, [1944] 2011.

______. *Early Vancouver, Vol. 7*. Vancouver: City of Vancouver, [1956] 2011.

Maynard, Robyn. *Policing Black Lives: State Violence in Canada from Slavery to the Present*. Halifax: Fernwood Publishing, 2017.

Smith, Lisa Anne, and Barbara Rogers. *Our Friend Joe: The Joe Fortes Story*. Vancouver: Ronsdale Press, 2012.

Tsang, Henry. *White Riot: The 1907 Anti-Asian Riots in Vancouver*. Vancouver: Arsenal Pulp Press, 2023.

Walcott, Rinaldo. *The Long Emancipation: Moving Toward Black Freedom*. Durham: Duke University Press, 2021.

INDEX

Page numbers in italics refer to photos/captions. Page numbers followed by "n" refer to footnotes.

A

ableism, 30n, 107
Abolition Act, 54
Active Pass, 35
Africa, 17, 66, 99
African descent, 52n, 53–54, 62, 88, 113
African Estadounidenses*, 52, 54–55, 57, 86
Afro Latine descent, 13–14, 20, 51, 55, 57–58, 66, 79–80, 113
Afrocaribeños, 13
After Canaan (Compton), 61
ageism, 30n
Alberta, 79
Alhambra Hotel, 43–44, 71–72
American Civil War, 55
American Revolutionary War, 53
Americas, 25, 52n, 66
amiskwaciy (Edmonton), 23, 33, 59, 79
Anderson, James, 104
Anderson, William C., 27–29, 34
anti-Asian racism, 38, 76, 92, 101
Anti-Asian Riots, 68, 73, *73*
anti-Black racism, 42, 78, 112
  colourism, 63
  dehumanization, 30n, 42, 52n, 64–66, 89
  legal, 29–30, 30n, 113
  mixed-race relationships, 98–99
  overcriminalization, 43n, 52, 52n, 54n
  in police force, 46
  slurs, 33, 61, 67, 67n, 70, 79, 85, 97, 113
  stereotypes, 52–53, 55–57, 59, 62, 78, 98
  systemic, 72, 85
  violence, 28–32, 53, 75n, 82, 85, 89, 99, 108
archivists, 37n
Argentina, 24
Aryan Guard, 80
Asian communities, 100
  migration, 83–84, 92
Asian descent, 73, 76
Astor, 78
Atlantic Ocean, 23–24

B

Baartman, Saartjie, 65–65
Baboth, Changich, 32–33
Backhouse, Constance, 99
Barbadian descent, 63
Barbadian-Creole descent, 54
Barbados, 29–30
Bérubé, Allan, 100
Birth of a Nation, The (Dixon Jr.), 75n
Black Belt, 81–82
Black communities, 38n, 51–53, 55, 59–60, 63–64, 72, 75n, 92, 104. *See also* Howard family; Scurry family
  anti-Black racism (*see* anti-Black racism)
  histories and legacies, 11–12, 51–52

Black communities continued
men in the nineteenth century, 23–24
migration, 53–54, 79–80
settlers, 43, 55n†
Black History Month, 11, 13, 112
Black Loyalists, 53
Black Southern (US) accent, 57, 72n
Blackness, 61–64, 109
Bodega Hotel, 67–68
Bolster, Jeff, 24, 31
Brasil, 24, 27
British Columbia, 54–55, 67, 84
British Crown, 24–25, 79
British descent, 53
British Empire, 18, 24–25, 30, 35, 42, 53–54, 66–67, 79
British Properties, 38
British West Indies, 25, 66–67
Brown Skin Beach, 44
Bruce, Charlie, 63
Burke (vice-consul), 71–72, 81
Burns, Tommy, 76, 77

C

cabin, 47, 88, 109–110, *111*
cacao industry, 20, 24
California, 54–55, 55n†
Cambie Street, 86
Canada, 53–54, 54n, 66, 73–74, 75n
Canada Post, 112
Canboulay riots, 21
Cape Horn, 26, 27–28
Capilano Reserve (X̱wemelch'stn), 47
capitalism, 24, 107
carding, 43n
Caribbean, 17, 19, 23, 53, 58, 62, 66–67, 81, 99
Caribbean descent, 55
Caribbean Sea, 18
Carrall Street, 78
Carrol, Thompson, and Mckenzie household, 86, 88–89
Catholic Church, 18–19, 80, 84, 86
Central America, 52n, 62
Chauvin, Derek, 85
Chen, Annie, 112
Chicago Tribune, 98
Chile, 17, 58–59
Chinatown, 38, 73
Chinese community, 37–38, 48, 76, 81, 83, 90–92, 94–96
Chinese Immigration Act, 83
City of Edmonton, 96
City of Vancouver, 38n, 45–47, 84, 92, 104–105
City of Vancouver Archives, 11, 20–21, 89
Clansman, The (Dixon Jr.), 73–74, 74, 75
Clarke, Arthur Bruce, 46
coffee industry, 20
College of Physicians and Surgeons of Alberta, 30
Colombo, Cristoforo, 18
colonialism, 18–19, 20, 30, 32, 35–36, 55, 59–60, 65–68, 96
colonization, 66, 79–80, 99, 103
colourism, 63
Compton, Wayde, 61–62
Confederation, 83
constable, special, 45–46, 48, 91, 96
continuous voyage regulation, 83–84
Cook (consul), 71–72
cotton industry, 28–29, 31, 82
Crystal Pool, 44

D
Davie Street, 40
decolonization, 50n, 59
dehumanization, 30n, 42, 52n, 64–66, 89
Deighton, John "Gassy Jack," 43–44
Delgamuukw v. British Columbia, 84
Dene people, 79
Denman Street, 40, 93
displacement of Indigenous peoples, 37, 47–48, 84, 95
Dixon Jr., Thomas, 73–74
Doctrine of Discovery, 18–19, 86
Douglas, James, 54–55
Douglass, Frederick, 98
Dred Scott v. Sandford, 30
Dunsmuir Street, 104

E
Edgren, Robert W., *77*
Edmonton (amiskwaciy), 23, 33, 59, 79
Edwards, Edward, 27–29, 35
Emerson, John, 30
England, 80
English, 20–21, 58, 66, 72n
English Bay (Íýelshn), 12, 40–42, 47, 71–72, 90–91, 93–94
 images of, *16*, *38*, *39*, *56*, *90*
English Bay bathhouse, 90, 100–101
English Bay Beach, *56*, 89, 91, 95, 96
enslavement of Africans, 17–19, 25, 30n, 50n, 52n, 53–54, 54n, 58, 62, 89
 abolition in British Empire, 20, 25, 42–43, 53–54, 54n
Estadounidenses*, definition, 52n
eugenics, 94–96, 98
Europe, 24, 26
Europeans, 18, 25, 36, 79–80
Evening Record (Windsor), 71–72

F
Fairview, *38*
False Creek (X̱áywá7esks), *38*, 47
farming, 20, 24
First Narrows, 37
Floyd, George, 85
Fortes, Serafim "Joe"
 accent, 57, 72n
 autobiography, 57, 68, 114
 birthdate, 20, 20n
 Blackness, 61–64, 109
 cabin, 47, 88, 109–110, *111*
 family, 20–21, 23, 66, 103, 106
 funeral, 12, 104–106
 handwriting, *21*
 health, 35, 105, 107
 images of, 11–12, *16*, *39*, *56*, *70*, 89–90, *90*, *95*
 memorials, 63, 110–112
 name, 14, 105
 obituaries and tributes, 13, 103–104, 106–109
 religion, 44, 96–97, 104, 105
 salary, 40, 45–47, 73, 107
 self-identity, 55, 57–58, 66–68
 special constable, 45–46, 48, 91, 96
Foster, Stephen, 104
Fountain Chapel Church, 92
freedom, 54n
French descent, 53
Fugitive Slave Act, 54

G

Gastown, 43–44
gender binaries, 93–94, 100, 103
George, Rueben, 41
Glasgow, Scotland, 26
Global South, 52n
Globe, 98
Graham, MarieClaire, 20n
Grande Prairie, 29
Granville Street, 104
Granville township, 35
Great Fire, 71

H

Halifax, 93–94
Haras, Jill, 112
head tax, 83–84
Hogan's Alley, 12, 38, 38n, 44, 92
homophobia, 99–101
Homulchesan (Capilano), 37. *See also* X̱wemelch'stn (Capilano Reserve)
hooks, bell, 85–86
Howard family, 88
  Howard, Barbara, 12
  Howard, Catherine "Cassie," 57, 105, 109
  Howard, Goldvine, 57, 88, 105–106, 109
  Howard, Samuel, 57, 75n
Hudson, Peter James, 63, 76, 89
human trafficking, 20, 23–24, 29–30, 43, 50n, 53–54. *See also* enslavement of Africans
Humane Society, 71–72

I

Illuminated Address, 68, 106
immigration restrictions, 79–80, 83–84
Indian Act, 41, 83
Indian migrants, 101
Indigenous communities, 40–42, 44, 55n†, 71, 79, 81, 83–85
  children, kidnapping of, 41, 83–84 (*see also* residential schools)
  displacement of, 37, 47–48, 84, 96 (*see also* reserves)
Indigenous lands, theft of, 35–36, 40, 47, 55n†, 83. *See also* settler colonialism
Indigenous nations, 36, 50n, 55n†. *See also* specific nations
Indigenous peoples in Caribbean and South America, 18–19, 62
Industrial Revolution, 36
Irving Hotel, 78
Íy̓el̓shn (English Bay). *See* English Bay (Íy̓el̓shn)

J

Jamaica, 17–18, 59, 66–67
James, C.L.R., 81–82
Japanese community, 37–38
Japantown (Paueru Gai), 38, 73
Jewish community, 92
Joe (Haras), 112
Joe, Matthias, 37
Joe Fortes Seafood & Chop House, 112, 112n
Johnson, Jack, 76–79, 77

K

Kalinago people, 18
Kamloops, 109
Kennedy, Neil, 23
Khatsahlano, August Jack, 36–37, 49
Khoikhoi people, 65
Kitsilano Indian Reserve (Sen̓áḵw), 38, 49
Komagata Maru, 100–101
Ku Klux Klan, 32, 73–74, 75n, 77, 96, 98–99, 113
Kwa7xiliya, 43
Kwakwa̱ka̱'wakw territory, 55n†

L

labour, 18, 20, 23–24, 45–46, 53–54, 55n‡, 81–82, 107, 113
land/property ownership, 24, 36, 38, 96
Latin America, 53, 58
Latine, 20, 58
Latinidad, 59
Lewis, Nya, 52
lifeguarding, 12, 44–47, 70, 72, 81, 89, 93
Lions Gate Bridge, 47
Liu, Yilong (Louie), 101
Liu-Trujillo, Robert, 11
Liverpool, England, 23–26, 57, 106
logging industry, 24, 37, 44
London, 65
Long Emancipation, The (Walcott), 54n
Lord Byng Secondary School, 32
Lorde, Audre, 59n
"Lost Tribe of a Lost Tribe, The" (Hudson), 63
Lower Mainland, 37, 76
Lubicon Nation, 36

M

Maclean's, 94–96
Maroons of Jamaica, 50n
Marsh, Leonard, 44, 92
Matthews, James Skitt, 35–37, 40, 93
Maynard, Robyn, 89
McBride, Richard, 47
McLean, Alec, 110
Métis people, 79
Metropole, 78
Mi'kmaq people, 53
Minja, Lara, 112
Minneapolis, 85
Mohawk people, 84
Murphy, Emily, 94–96
Museum of Man, 65–66
Musqueam (xʷməθkʷəy̓əm) Nation, 35, 37

N

Nanaimo Street, 92
National Day for Truth and Reconciliation, 84
National Film Board of Canada, 112
Neelander, Thomas, 45
"Negro," 11, 29–30, 43, 51, 61
Nêhiyaw people, 79
NHL, 85
Niitsitapi people, 79
North America, 19, 25, 52n
Nova Scotia, 53

O

"Old Black Joe" (Foster), 15, 104, 109
Ontario, 53, 86
Our Friend Joe (Smith and Rogers), 32, 40
Our Lady of the Holy Rosary Cathedral, 97, 104
overcriminalization, 43n, 52, 52n, 54n

P
Pacific coastline, 26
Panamá, 26
Paris, 65
Paris, George, 78
Park Lane, 92
passing, 61–62
Patois, 20–21, 57, 114
pheneticizing, 61–62, 89–90
pieza, 30n
Pitts, Helen, 98
plantations, 20–21, 23–25, 29–30, 32, 50n, 53, 66, 81–82, 105
police, 43n, 52, 52n, 54n, 84–85, 100–101, 104–105
Policing Black Lives (Maynard), 89
Polish descent, 59
Portuguese community, 37
Portuguese descent, 20, 63
Prairies, 79–80
Prince Edward Island, 53
prospecting, 44, 55
Punjabi, 100–101

Q
Quebec, 53
Quw'utsun territory, 55, 55n†

R
racial segregation, 13, 25, 37–38, 43–45, 46–47, 48, 76, 83, 89, 91–94
racial slurs, 33, 61, 67, 67n, 70, 79, 85, 97, 113
racial stereotypes, 52–53, 55–57, 59, 62, 78, 98
racialized communities, 71, 83, 92–93. *See also* specific communities
Rainier, 78
reserves, 37, 47–48, 79, 83
residential schools, 19, 83–84
Rex v. Singh, 101
River Mersey, 25, 100
Rivers, Khelsilem, 47
Robert Kerr, 26–30, 32, 34–35
Robinson, Noel, 63–65, 68
Rogers, Barbara, 14–15, 32, 40
Royal Canadian Mounted Police, 84. *See also* police

S
Saggers, D., 110
Salt Spring Island, 55, 55n†
Sammons, Jeffrey, 79
San Francisco, 100
San Juan Island, 35
Scott, Dred, 30
Scottish descent, 54
Scramble for Africa, 36
Scurry family, 57, 86–88
- Scurry, Charles, 75n
- Scurry, Hiram, 57, 86–87
- Scurry, Martha, 57, 86–88, 106, 109

seafaring, 23–24, 26–32, 43–44, 67
Seṅáḵw, 44, 47, 84, 96
settler colonialism, 35–36, 40–41, 44, 48, 69, 83, 86, 91, 100
sexuality, 24, 96–97, 99–101
səlilwətaɬ (Tsleil-Waututh) Nation, 35, 37, 41
Shelburne, Nova Scotia, 54
Sikh communities, 100–101
Sing, 91–92
Singh, Dalip and Naina, 100–101
Sinixt Nation, 36
skin tones, 61–64. *See also* colourism
Skrewdriver, 80–82
Sḵwx̱wú7mesh (Squamish) Nation, 35–37, 40–41, 43–44, 47–48, 84
Slave Codes, 29–30, 107
smallpox, 41
Smith, Lisa Anne, 14–15, 32, 40

Smith Díaz, Ruby, *16, 111*
South Africa, 65
South America, 19, 24, 25, 26, 52n, 62, 99
South Asia, 84
South Asian community, 37, 84
 migration, 101
South Vancouver, 38
Southern United States, 52, 57, 98, 105
Spain, 18, 62
Spanish, 20–21, 57–58, 66, 114
Spanish descent, 20, 62, 113
speculative archiving, 20n
Spotts, Fielding, 12
Squamish (Sḵwx̱wú7mesh) Nation, 35–37, 40–41, 43–44, 47–48, 84
St. Francis Hotel, 77–78
Stanley Park (X̱wáýx̱way), 37, 42, 84
Stoney Nakoda, 79
Stz'uminus territory, 55, 55n†
sugar cane industry, 20–21, 24, 25
Supreme Court of Canada, 36
Supreme Court of the United States, 30
swimming, 13, 25–26, 44–46, 71–73, 94, 95, 96–97
Sydney, Australia, 76

T

Taíno people, 18
Tekahionwake (E. Pauline Johnson), 84
terra nullius, 36, 38, 48, 60
Texas, USA, 76
Thanksgiving, 72
Ting, Carson, 112
tobacco industry, 25, 31
Toronto, Canada, 106
Trinidad (Kairi), 12–13, 17–18, 20, 23, 35, 48, 57, 63, 66–67
Tsleil-Waututh (səlilwətaɬ) Nation, 35, 37, 41
Turtle Island, 17, 33, 36, 51, 54n, 61, 81, 85, 99

U

Ukrainian descent, 59
UN Declaration on the Rights of Indigenous Peoples, 84
United States, 23, 25, 30, 52n, 53–54, 54n, 73–74, 75n, 85, 104–105. *See also* Southern United States

V

Vancouver, George, 36
Vancouver Athletic Club, 76, 78
Vancouver Census, 20, 55
Vancouver Daily Province, 72, 78, 88, 106–108, 110
Vancouver Daily World, 26
Vancouver Heritage Foundation, 70n
Vancouver Historical Society, 112
Vancouver International Airport, 84
Vancouver Island, 54
Vancouver Morgue, 108
Vancouver Mural Festival, 112
Vancouver Opera House, 73–74
Vancouver Park Board, 110
Vancouver Police Department, 45–46, 96, 104. *See also* police
Vancouver Public Library, 110
Vancouver School Board, 12
Vancouver Sun, *102*, 108, 109–110
Vancouver township, 37
Vanier Park, 84
Vatican, 19, 86
Venezuela, 18, 20
Victoria, 26, 55

W

Wainborn, George, *111*
Walcott, Rinaldo, 54n
Walker, James W.St.G., 43
Wallen, Morgan, 85
War of 1812, 53
Wessels, Wynand, 30
West Coast, 44, 100
West End, 110, 112–113
West End forest, 42, 88
West Indian descent, 55n‡, 63
West Indian Domestic Scheme, 55
West Indies, 25, 66–67
West Vancouver, 38
Wet'suwet'en Nation, 84
white gaze, 14–15, 51, 58–59, 62–64, 66–69, 71–72, 88
white settlers, 41–43, 54, 68, 91–92, 103
  social status from proximity to Blackness, 45, 89
white supremacy, 13–15, 24–25, 30–31, 42, 58–59, 73, 79–80, 88, 92, 94–96, 98–99, 108
Whitzman, Carolyn, 97
Whoi-Whoi (Lumberman's Arch), 37
Whyte Avenue, 33
Winnipeg, 86
Woman's Christian Temperance Union, 93–94
World War II, 55
W̱SÁNEĆ territory, 55, 55n†

X

X̱ats'alanexw (Kitsilano), 47
X̱áywá7esks (False Creek), *38*, 47
X̱wáýx̱way (Stanley Park), 42, 84
X̱wemelch'stn (Capilano Reserve), 47
xʷməθkʷəy̓əm (Musqueam) Nation, 35, 37

RUBY SMITH DÍAZ is a multidisciplinary artist, educator, and award-winning body positive personal trainer. She was born to Chilean and Jamaican parents in amiskwaciy (Edmonton) and graduated from the University of Alberta with a degree in education with distinction. Ruby's experiences of marginalization as a youth have inspired her to dedicate her life's work to equity and social justice. Her artistic work has been featured in the Vancouver International Film Festival, the Art Gallery of Greater Victoria, the Contemporary Art Gallery of Vancouver, and Mount Saint Vincent University Art Gallery. She currently resides on unceded Stz'uminus territory (Ladysmith, BC). | *tierranegraarts.ca*